Henry Clay Trumbull

The covenant of salt as based on the significance and symbolism of salt in primitive thought

Henry Clay Trumbull

The covenant of salt as based on the significance and symbolism of salt in primitive thought

ISBN/EAN: 9783337714710

Printed in Europe, USA, Canada, Australia, Japan

Cover: Foto ©ninafisch / pixelio.de

More available books at **www.hansebooks.com**

THE

COVENANT OF SALT

AS BASED ON THE SIGNIFICANCE AND SYMBOLISM OF SALT IN PRIMITIVE THOUGHT

BY

H. CLAY TRUMBULL

Author of "The Blood Covenant," "The Threshold Covenant," "Kadesh-barnea," "Studies in Oriental Social Life," etc.

NEW YORK
CHARLES SCRIBNER'S SONS
1899

PREFACE

In 1884 I issued a volume on "The Blood Covenant: A Primitive Rite and its Bearings on Scripture." Later I was led to attempt, and to announce as in preparation, another volume in the field of primitive covenants, including a treatment of "The Name Covenant," "The Covenant of Salt," and "The Threshold Covenant." In 1896, I issued a separate volume on "The Threshold Covenant," that subject having grown into such prominence in my studies as to justify its treatment by itself. These two works, "The Blood Covenant" and "The Threshold Covenant," have been welcomed by scholars on both sides of the ocean to an extent beyond my expectations, and in view of this I venture to submit some further researches in the field of primitive thought and customs.

Before the issuing of my second volume, I had prepared the main portion of this present work on "The Covenant of Salt," but since then I have been led to revise it, and to conform it more fully to my latest conclusion as to the practical identity of all covenants. It is in this form that I present it, as a fresh contribution to the study of archeology and of anthropology.

As I have come to see it, as a result of my researches, the very idea of a "covenant" in primitive thought is a union of being, or of persons, in a common life, with the approval of God, or of the gods. This was primarily a sharing of blood, which is life, between two persons, through a rite which had the sanction of him who is the source of all life. In this sense "blood brotherhood" and the "threshold covenant" are but different forms of one and the same *covenant*. The blood of animals shared in a common sacrifice is counted as the blood which makes two one in a sacred covenant. Wine as "the blood of the grape" stands for the blood which is the life of all flesh; hence the sharing of wine stands for the sharing of blood or life. So, again, salt represents blood, or life, and the covenant of salt is simply another form of the one blood covenant. This is the main point of this new monograph. So far as I know, this truth has not before been recognized or formulated.

Similarly the sharing of a common name, especially of the name of God, or of a god, is the claim of a divinely sanctioned covenant between those who bear it. It is another mode of claiming to be in the one vital covenant. A temporary agreement, or truce, between two who share a drink of water or a morsel of bread, is a lesser and very different thing from entering into a covenant, which by its very nature is permanent and unchangeable. This difference is pointed out and emphasized in the following pages.

In these new investigations, as in my former ones, I have been aided, step by step, by specialists, who have kindly given me suggestions and assistance by every means in their power. This furnishes a fresh illustration of the readiness of all scholars to aid any fresh worker in any line where their own labors render them an authority or a guide.

Besides my special acknowledgments in the text and footnotes of this volume, I desire to express my indebtedness and thanks to these scholars who have freely rendered me important assistance at various points in my studies : Professor Dr. Hermann V. Hilprecht, the Rev. Drs. Marcus Jastrow, K. Kohler, and Henry C. McCook, Professor Drs. Hermann Collitz, H. Carrington Bolton, William H. Roberts, Morris Jastrow, Jr., F. K. Sanders, William A. Lamberton, W. W. Keen, William Osler, J. W. Warren, and D. C. Munro, Drs. J. Solis Cohen, Thomas G. Morton, Charles W. Dulles, Henry C. Cattell, and Frederic H. Howard, Rev. Dean E. T. Bartlett, President Robert E. Thompson, Drs. Talcott Williams, Henry C. Lea, and T. H. Powers Sailer, Messrs. Clarence H. Clark and Patterson Du Bois.

This third work is to be considered in connection with the two which have preceded it in the same field. It is hoped that it will be recognized as adding an important thought to the truths brought out in those works severally.

A previously published monograph on "The Ten Commandments as a Covenant of Love" is added to "The Covenant of Salt" as a Supplement, in order that it may be available to readers of this series of volumes on covenants, as a historical illustration of the subject under discussion.

H. C. T.

PHILADELPHIA,
    October, 1899.

CONTENTS

I.
CHARACTERISTICS OF A COVENANT 1

II.
A COVENANT OF SALT 11

III.
BIBLE REFERENCES TO THE RITE 15

IV.
BREAD AND SALT 21

V.
SALT REPRESENTING BLOOD 35

VI.
SALT REPRESENTING LIFE 51

VII.
SALT AND SUN, LIFE AND LIGHT 71

VIII.
SIGNIFICANCE OF BREAD 77

IX.
SALT IN SACRIFICES 81

X.
SALT IN EXORCISM AND DIVINATION 97

XI.
FAITHLESSNESS TO SALT 107

XII.
SUBSTITUTE TOGETHER WITH REALITY 115

XIII.
ADDED TRACES OF THE RITE 121

XIV.
A SAVOR OF LIFE OR OF DEATH 131

XV
MEANS OF A MERGED LIFE 139

SUPPLEMENT
THE TEN COMMANDMENTS AS A COVENANT OF LOVE . 143

INDEXES
TOPICAL INDEX, 177.   SCRIPTURAL INDEX, 183.

1
CHARACTERISTICS OF A COVENANT

I

CHARACTERISTICS OF A COVENANT

Our English word "covenant," like many another word in our language and in other languages, fails to convey, or even to contain, its fullest and most important meaning in comparison with the idea back of it. As a matter of fact, this must be true of nearly all words. Ideas precede words. Ideas have spirit and life before they are shaped or clothed in words. Words have necessarily human limitations and imperfectness, because of their purely human origin.

When an idea first seeks expression in words, it is inevitable that it be cramped by the means employed for its conveyance. At the best the word can only *suggest* the idea back of it, rather than accurately *define* and explain that idea. In practice, or in continued and varied use, in the development of thought and of language, changes necessarily occur in the word or words selected to convey a primal idea, in order to indicate other phases of the idea than that brought out or pointed to by the first chosen word.

While these changes and additions aid some persons to an understanding of the root idea, they tend to confuse others, especially those who are looking for exactness of definition.

As a rule, the earlier words chosen for the expression of an idea are more likely than later ones to suggest the main thought seeking expression. Hence there is often a gain in looking back among the Greek and Sanskrit and Hebrew and Assyrian roots carried forward by religion or commerce into our English words and idioms, when we are searching for the true meaning of an important custom or rite or thought. Yet this will ordinarily be confusing rather than clarifying to an exact scholar. Only as a person is intent on the primal thought back of the chosen word is he likely to perceive the true meaning and value of the suggestions of the earlier word or words found in his searching.

Archeology is sometimes more valuable than philology in throwing light on the meaning of ancient words. It is often easier to explain the use of an archaic word by a disclosed primitive custom or rite, than to discern a hidden primitive rite or custom by a study of the words used in referring to it. An archeologist may suggest a solution of a problem which hopelessly puzzles the lexicographer or grammarian. Sentiment and the poetic instinct are often more helpful, in such research, than prescribed etymological methods. He who looks for an exact definition can never reach a conclusion. If he seeks a suggestion, he may find one.

"Covenant," as an English word, simply means, according to its etymological signification, "a coming together." At times the word is used interchangeably with such words as "an agreement," "a league," "a treaty," "a compact," "an arrangement," "an obligation," or "a promise." Only by its context and connections are we shown in special cases that a covenant bond has peculiar or pre-eminent sacredness and perpetuity. This truth is, however, shown in many an instance, especially in translations from earlier languages.

Even in our use of the English word "covenant" we have to recognize, at times, its meaning as a sacred and indissoluble joining together of the two parties covenanting, as distinct from any ordinary agreement or compact. And when we go back, as in our English Bible, to the Greek and Hebrew words rendered "covenant," or "testament," or "oath," in a sworn bond, we find this distinction more strongly emphasized. It is therefore essential to a correct view of any form of primitive covenanting that we understand the root idea in this primal sort of coming together.

Primitive covenanting was by two persons cutting into each other's flesh, and sharing by contact, or by drinking, the blood thus brought out. Earliest it was the personal blood of the two parties that was the nexus of their covenant. Later it was the blood of a shared and eaten sacrifice that formed the covenant nexus. In such a case the food of the feast became a part of the life of each and both, and fixed their union. In any case it was the common life into which each party was brought by the covenant that bound them irrevocably. This fixed the binding of the two as permanent and established.[1]

Lexicographers and critics puzzle over the supposed Hebrew or Assyrian origin of the words translated "covenant" in our English Bible, and they fail to agree even reasonably well on the root or roots involved. Yet all the various words or roots suggested by them have obvious reference to the primal idea of covenanting as a means of life-sharing; therefore their verbal differences are, after all, of minor importance, and may simply point to different stages in the progressive development of the languages.

Whether, therefore, the root of the Hebrew *bĕreeth*

---

[1] See *Blood Covenant* and *Threshold Covenant*, passim.

means, as is variously claimed, "to cut," "to fetter," "to bind together," "to fix," "to establish," "to pour out," or "to eat," it is easy to see how these words may have been taken as referring to the one primitive idea of a compassed and established union.¹ So in the Greek words *diathēkē* and *horkion* it can readily be seen that the references to the new placing or disposing of the parties, to their solemn appeal to God or the gods in the covenanting, and to the testament to take effect after the death of the testator, or to the means employed in this transaction, are alike consistent with the primitive idea of a covenant in God's sight by which one gives over one's very self, or one's entire possessions, to another. The pledged or merged personality of the two covenantors fully accounts for the different suggested references of the variously employed words.

True marriage is thus a covenant, instead of an arrangement. The twain become no longer two, but one; each is given to the other; their separate identity is lost in their common life. A ring, a bracelet, a band, has been from time immemorial the symbol and pledge of such an indissoluble union.²

---

[1] See Gesenius's *Hebraeisches und Aramaeisches Wörterbuch*, 12th ed., p. 120; Norwach's *Lehrbuch der Hebraeischen Archaeologie*, I., p. 358, note 1; Friedrich Delitzsch's *The Hebrew Language Viewed in the Light of Assyrian Research*, p. 41; *Blood Covenant*, 2d ed., p. 264.

[2] *Blood Covenant*, 2d ed., pp. 54, 75, 77.

Men have thus, many times and in many ways, signified their covenanting, and their consequent interchange of personality and of being, by the exchange of certain various tokens and symbols; but these exchanges have not in any sense been the covenant itself, they have simply borne witness to a covenant. Thus men have exchanged pledges of their covenant to be worn as phylacteries, or caskets, or amulets, or belts, on neck, or forehead, or arm, or body;[1] they have exchanged weapons of warfare or of the chase; they have exchanged articles of ordinary dress, or of ornament, or of special utility;[2] they have exchanged with each other their personal names.[3] All these have been in token of an accomplished covenant, but they have not been forms or rites of the covenant itself.

Circumcision is spoken of in the Old Testament as the token of a covenant between the individual and God. It is so counted by the Jew and the Muhammadan. In Madagascar, as illustrative of outside nations, it is counted as the token of a covenant between the individual and his earthly sovereign. The ceremonies accompanying it all go to prove this.[4] Again,

---

[1] *Blood Covenant*, 2d ed., pp. 232-238, 326-330.
[2] *Ibid.*, pp. 14, 24, 28, 35 f., 62, 270; 1 Sam. 18:4; 20:1-13.
[3] *Ibid.*, 2d ed., p. 334 f.
[4] *Ibid.* pp. 215-233; Gen. 17:1-14; Ellis's *History of Madagascar*, pp. 176-186.

men have covenanted with one another to merge their common interests, and to obliterate or ignore their racial, tribal, or social distinctions, as no mere treaty or league could do.

In tradition and in history men have covenanted with God, or with their gods, so that they could claim and bear the divine name as their own, thus sharing and representing the divine personality and power.[1] Thus also in tradition different gods of primitive peoples and times have covenanted with one another, so that each was the other, and the two were the same.[2]

There are seeming traces of this root idea of covenanting, through making two one by merging the life of each in a common life, in words that make "union" out of "one." In the Welsh *un* is "one;" *uno* is "to unite." In the English, from the Latin, a unit unites with another unit, and the two are unified in the union. The two by this merging become not a *double*, but a larger *one*. Thus it is always in a true covenant.

We have to study the meaning and growth of words in the light of ascertained primitive customs and rites and ideas, instead of expecting to learn from ascertained root-words what were the prevailing primal

---

[1] *Blood Covenant*, 2d ed., p. 335.
[2] See Trumbull's *Friendship the Master-Passion*, p. 73 f.

ideas and rites and customs in the world. In the line of such studying, covenants and the covenant relation have been found to be an important factor, and to have had a unique significance in the development of human language and in the progress of the human race from its origin and earliest history. The study and disclosures of the primitive covenant idea in its various forms and aspects have already brought to light important truths and principles, and the end is not yet.

II
A COVENANT OF SALT

II

A COVENANT OF SALT

Among the varied forms of primitive covenanting, perhaps none is more widely known and honored, or less understood, the world over, than a covenant of salt, or a salt covenant. Religion and superstition, civilization and barbarism, alike deal with it as a bond or rite, yet without making clear the reasons for its use. The precise significance and symbolism of salt as the nexus of a lasting covenant is by no means generally understood or clearly defined by even scholars and scientists. The subject is certainly one worthy of careful consideration and study.

A covenant of salt has mention, in peculiar relations, in the Bible. It is prominent in the literature and traditions of the East. Here in our Western world there are various folk-lore customs and sayings that show familiarity with it as a vestige of primitive thought. Among the islands of the sea, and in out-of-the-way corners of the earth, it shows itself as clearly as in Europe, Asia, Africa, and America.

In some regions salt is spoken of as if it were merely an accompaniment of bread, and thus a common and indispensable article of food ; but, again, its sharing stands out as signifying far more than is meant by an ordinary meal or feast. An explanation of its meaning, frequently offered or accepted by students and specialists, is that in its nature it is a preservative and essential, and therefore its presence adds value to an offering or to a sacramental rite.[1] But the mind cannot be satisfied with so superficial an interpretation as this, in view of many things in text and tradition that go to show a unique sacredness of salt as salt, rather than as a preserver and enlivener of something that is of more value. It is evident that the true symbolism and sanctity of salt as the nexus of a covenant lie deeper than is yet admitted, or than has been formally stated by any scholar.

[1] See W. Robertson Smith's *Religion of the Semites*, pp. 203, 252 ; Art. "Salt," by W. R. S. in *Encyc. Brit.;* Trumbull's *Studies in Oriental Social Life*, pp. 106-112, with citations ; Norwach's *Lehrbuch der Hebræischen Archæologie*, II, p. 245, etc.

III
BIBLE REFERENCES TO THE RITE

III

BIBLE REFERENCES TO THE RITE

A "covenant of salt" seems to stand quite by itself in the Bible record. Covenants made in blood, and again as celebrated by sharing a common meal, and by the exchange of weapons and clothing, and in various other ways, are of frequent mention; but a covenant of salt is spoken of only three times, and in every one of these cases as if it were of peculiar and sacred significance; each case is unique.

The Lord speaks of his covenant with Aaron and his sons, in the privileges of the priesthood in perpetuity, as such a covenant. To him he says: "All the heave offerings of the holy things, which the children of Israel offer unto the Lord, have I given thee, and thy sons and thy daughters with thee, as a due for ever: it is a *covenant of salt* for ever before the Lord unto thee and to thy seed with thee."[1]

Of the Lord's covenant with David and his seed, in the rights and privileges of royalty, Abijah the king of

---

[1] Num. 18 : 19.

Judah says to Jeroboam, the rival king of Israel: "O Jeroboam and all Israel; ought ye not to know that the Lord, the God of Israel, gave the kingdom over Israel to David for ever, even to him and to his sons by a *covenant of salt?*"[1]

Again, the Lord, through Moses, enjoins it upon the people of Israel to be faithful in the offering of sacrifices at his altar, according to the prescribed ritual. "Neither shalt thou suffer the *salt of the covenant* of thy God," he says, "to be lacking from thy meal offering: with all thine oblations thou shalt offer salt."[2]

While the word "covenant" appears more than two hundred and fifty times in the Old Testament, it is a remarkable fact that the term "covenant of salt" occurs in only these three instances, and then in such obviously exceptional connections. The Lord's covenant with Aaron and his seed in the priesthood, and with David and his seed in the kingship, is as a covenant of salt, perpetual and unalterable. And God's people in all their holy offerings are to bear in mind that the salt is a vital element and factor, if they would come within the terms of the perpetual and unalterable covenant.

In the Bible, God speaks to men by means of

---

[1] 2 Chron. 13: 5.   [2] Lev. 2: 13.

human language; and in the figures of speech which he employs he makes use of terms which had and have a well-known significance among men. His employment of the term "covenant of salt" as implying permanency and unchangeableness to a degree unknown to men, except in a covenant of blood as a covenant of very life, is of unmistakable significance.

There are indeed incidental references, in another place in the Old Testament, to the prevailing primitive idea that salt-sharing is covenant-making. These references should not be overlooked.

In many lands, and in different ages, salt has been considered the possession of the government, or of the sovereign of the realm, to be controlled by the ruler, as a source of life, or as one of its necessaries, for his people. In consequence of this the receiving of salt from the king's palace has been deemed a fresh obligation of fidelity on the part of his subjects. This is indicated in a Bible passage with reference to the rebuilding by Zerubbabel of the Temple at Jerusalem. under the edict of Cyrus, king of Persia. "The adversaries of Judah and Benjamin" protested against the work as a seditious act. In giving their reason for this course they said : "Now because we eat the salt of the palace [because we are bound to the king by a covenant of salt], and it is not meet for us to see the king's dishonor, therefore have we sent and certified the king."[1]

And so again when King Darius showed his confidence in the Jews by directing a supply, from the royal treasury, of material for sacrifices at the Temple, and a renewal of the means of covenanting, he declared: "Moreover I make a decree what ye shall do to these elders of the Jews for the building of this house of God: that of the king's goods, even of the tribute beyond the river, expenses be given with all diligence unto these men, that they be not hindered. And that which they have need of, both young bullocks, and rams, and lambs, for burnt offerings to the God of heaven, wheat, salt, wine, and oil, according to the word of the priests which are at Jerusalem, let it be given them day by day without fail: that they may offer sacrifices of sweet savor unto the God of heaven, and pray for the life of the king, and of his sons."[2] And again, in further detail: "Unto an hundred talents of silver, and to an hundred measures of wheat, and to an hundred baths of wine, and to an hundred baths of oil, and salt without prescribing how much;"[3] the more salt they took, the more surely and firmly they were bound.

[1] Ezra 4:14.   [2] Ezra 6:8-10.   [3] Ezra 7:22.

IV
BREAD AND SALT

IV

BREAD AND SALT

"There would be nothing eatable," says Plutarch, "without salt, which, mixed with flour, seasons bread also. Hence it was that Neptune and Ceres [or Poseidon and Demeter as the Greeks called them] had both the same temple."[1] And from the days of Plutarch until now, as has been already mentioned, it has been customary to speak of the "covenant of salt" as synonymous with the "covenant of bread and salt;" or as identical with the covenant of food-sharing in the rite of hospitality. But the covenant of salt among primitive peoples has, and ever has had, a sacredness and depth of meaning far beyond what is involved in the ordinary sharing of food.

Even the sharing of water between two persons, or the giving and receiving of a drink of water, is a compact of peace for the time being, as a truce between enemies.[2] The sharing of bread, or of flesh, means yet

---
[1] Plutarch's *Sympos.* (Goodwin's edition), Book IV. Ques. IV., § 3.
[2] See Trumbull's *Studies in Oriental Social Life*, pp. 361-363.

more than the sharing of water. It brings those who join in it into the league or treaty of hospitality, by which the host is pledged to his guest while he is a guest, and for a reasonable time after his departure.[1]

Durzee Bey, a native chieftain in Mesopotamia, having put a bit of roast meat into the mouth of Dr. Hamlin, as they sat together in his domicil, said: "By that act I have pledged you every drop of my blood, that *while you are in my territory* no evil shall come to you. *For that space of time* we are brothers."[2] "Where enmity subsists, the fiercer Arabs will not sit down at the same table with their adversary; sitting down together betokens reconciliation."[3]

A covenant of salt is, however, permanent and unalterable, as the truce or treaty is not. Yet this distinction, recognized by Orientals, does not seem to be

---

[1] See Burckhardt's *Travels in Syria*, p. 294 f.; *Beduinen und Wahaby*, p. 144 f.; Niebuhr's *Beschreibung von Arabien*, p. 48; Lane's *The Thousand and One Nights*, II., 423, note 21; Wetzstein's *Sprachliches*, p. 28 f.; Denham and Clapperton's *Travels and Discoveries in Africa*, p. xli; Warburton's *The Crescent and the Cross*, fifth ed., II., 167 f.; Pierrotti's *Customs and Traditions of Palestine*, p. 210 f.; Burton's *Pilgrimage to El Medinah and Meccah*, III., 86; Thomson's *The Land and the Book*, II., 40-43; Merrill's *East of the Jordan*, pp. 488-491; Harmer's *Observations*, fifth ed., I., 388 f.; Doughty's *Travels in Arabian Deserts*, I., 228; *Studies in Oriental Social Life*, pp. 73-142; W. Robertson Smith's *Kinship and Marriage in Early Arabia*, p. 149 f. Compare also Gen. 24 : 12-14; Deut. 23 : 3, 4; 1 Sam. 25 : 10, 11; 1 Kings 18 : 4; Job 22 : 7; Matt. 10 : 42; Mark 9 : 41; John 4 : 9.

[2] Hamlin's *Among the Turks*, p. 175 f.

[3] Russell's *Natural History of Aleppo*, Book II., chap. 4 (I., 232).

observed by all writers on Oriental customs, even by those who are generally observant and experienced.

It is true that the sharing of salt is usually an accompaniment of bread-sharing; hence, a covenant of salt between two parties is generally, although not always, made by their partaking of bread and salt together. Moreover, because salt is a common ingredient in Oriental bread, the eating of bread with another in the East may include the sharing of salt with him; but in such a case it is the salt, and not the bread, which is the nexus of the perpetual covenant, in its distinction from the temporary compact of hospitality in the sharing of bread. The bread is the vehicle of the covenant-making salt. Indeed, they have it for a proverb among Arabs and Syrians, "My bread had no salt in it," as a mode of accounting for any act of treachery, or failure in fidelity toward one who was a partaker of the bread of hospitality.

In the famous Oriental story of "Ali Baba and the Forty Thieves," the captain of the robber band who had visited Ali Baba in order to murder him was unwilling to partake of any food which had salt in it. This carefulness it was that excited the suspicion of Morgiana, the faithful slave girl, and led her to ask, "Who is he that eateth [only] meat wherein is no salt?" And when she recognized the robber captain under his disguise, she said to herself: "So ho ! this is the cause why the villain eateth not of salt, for that he seeketh now an opportunity to slay my master, whose mortal enemy he is."[1] This man was ready enough to partake of bread and flesh as a guest, and then strike his host to the heart in violation of all the obligations of hospitality; as, indeed, has been done in many a case in the East in early and in recent times,[2] but he could not consent, robber and murderer as he was, to disregard a sacred "covenant of salt."

The story of the origin of the dynasty of the Saffaride Kaleefs, in the ninth century, is an illustration of the surpassing power of the covenant of salt. Laiss-el-Safar, or Laiss the coppersmith, was an obscure worker in brass and copper, in Khorassan, a province of Persia. His son Yakoob wrought for a time at his father's trade, and then became a robber chieftain.

Having on one occasion found his way by night through a subterranean passage into the treasury of the palace of the governor, Nassar Seyar, who was then in control of Seiestan, Yakoob gathered jewels and costly stuffs, and was proceeding to carry them

---

[1] Burton's *Thousand and One Nights*, "Supplemental Nights," III., 398 f.

[2] See, for example, Layard's account of the murder of a Koordish Bey by Ibrâheem Agha, after the latter had risen from the table of the former (*Nineveh and its Remains*, I., 96 f.) ; also his account of other murderous violations of the rites of hospitality (*Ibid.*, I., 107 f. ; *Nineveh and Babylon*, p. 38).

off. Striking his bare foot, in the darkness, against a hard and sharp substance on the floor of the room, he thought it might be a jewel, and stooped to pick it up. Putting it to his tongue, to test it after the manner of lapidaries, he discovered that it was rock salt that he had tasted in the governor's palace. At once he threw down his bale of stolen goods, and left the palace by the way he had entered.

The signs of attempted robbery being found the next morning, the governor caused a proclamation to be made throughout the city, that, if the man who had entered the treasury would make himself known at the palace, he should be pardoned, and should be shown marks of special favor. Yakoob accordingly presented himself at the palace, and freely told his story. The governor felt that a man who would hold thus sacred the covenant of salt could be depended on, and Yakoob was given a position near his person.

Step by step Yakoob went forward to power and honors, until he was chief ruler of Khorassan, and founder of the Saffaride dynasty in the Persian khaleefate. He died A.D. 878, and was succeeded by his brother, Omar II.[1]

Baron du Tott, the Hungarian French traveler among the Turks and Tatars, tells of his experience

[1] Price's *Mohammedan History*, II., 229 f.

in this line with one Moldovanji Pasha, who desired a closer intimacy than was practicable in the brief time the two were to be together. "I had already," says the Baron du Tott, "attended him halfway down the staircase [of my house], when stopping, and turning briskly to one of my domestics who followed me, 'Bring me directly,' said he, 'some bread and salt.' I was not less surprised at this fancy than at the haste which was made to obey him. What he requested was brought, when, taking a little salt between his fingers, and putting it with a mysterious air on a bit of bread, he ate it with a devout gravity, assuring me that I might now rely on him."[1]

Stephen Schultz, in his Travels through Europe, Asia, and Africa, gives this illustration of the binding force of the covenant of salt: "On the 13th of June [1754] the deacon, Joseph Diab, a custom-house clerk, was at table with us. Referring to the salt which stood on the table, he said that the Arabs make use of it as a token of friendship. While they are fond of it, they do not like to place it on the table. On one occasion, when he was with a caravan traveling to Babel [Bagdad], they came into a neighborhood where Arabs were encamped. In the caravan

---

[1] Baron du Tott's *Memoirs of the Turks and Tartars*, Part I., p. 214, quoted in Bush's *Illustrations of the Holy Scriptures*.

was a rich merchant. Seeing that one of the Arabs was making ready to come to the caravan, he buried his money in the ground, built a fire over it, and then sat down to eat with the others near the fire. When the Arabs arrived they were welcomed pleasantly, and invited to eat. They accepted the invitation and sat down at the table. But when their leader saw the salt on the table, he said to the merchant, 'My loss is your gain ; for as I have eaten at a table on which is salt, I cannot, must not, harm you.' When that caravan started on its way, the Arab leader not only refrained from taking what he had intended to demand, but he escorted them without reward as far as the Euphrates, and gave them over into the care of the Pasha of Bagdad, as friends of his prince Achsam. They were now safe."

Schultz adds : "It is not customary among Arabs to place salt on a common table, but only when an Arab prince enters into an alliance with a pacha, which is called *baret-millah*, or the salt alliance. This is done as follows : The Arab prince, when he wishes to live within the jurisdiction of a pacha sends messengers to him to ask whether he may dwell in his territory as an ally. If the pacha consents, he sends messengers to the prince, informing him that they will meet on such a day. When the day arrives the pacha rides out to meet the prince, in the field which he has selected for his dwelling, and conducts him to his own quarters. Then the Arab prince asks the pacha how much he is to pay for permission to dwell in that field. The bargain is soon concluded, according to the extent of the Arab encampment.

"As soon as the bargain is concluded, a repast is prepared, and a salt-cellar, with some pieces of bread on a flat dish, is carried round the apartment by the pacha's servants. The dish is first presented to the pacha, who takes a piece of bread, dips it in the salt, and, holding it between two fingers toward the prince, calls out, 'Salaam!' that is Peace, 'I am the friend of your friend, and the enemy of your enemy.' The dish is now presented to the Arab prince, who likewise takes a piece of bread, dips it in the salt, and says to the pacha, 'Peace! I am the friend of your friend, and the enemy of your enemy!' Thereupon the dish with the bread is handed to the chief men of the Arab prince, and to the ministers of the pacha, who receive it in the same manner as their principals; with the exception that they simply say, on taking the bread, 'Salaam!' 'Peace'"[1]

Don Raphel speaking of the "conventions," or

---

[1] Schultz's *Leitungen des Höchsten nach seinem Rath auf den Reisen durch Europa, Asia, und Afrika*, Part V., p. 246, quoted in Rosenmuller's *Des alte und neue Morgenland*, II., 152 f.

rather the "covenants," which are recognized by the Bed'ween as sacredly binding on them, says: "One kind of these conventions is made by their putting some grains of salt with pieces of bread into each other's mouths, saying, 'By the rite of bread and salt,' or, 'By this salt and bread, I will not betray thee.' No oath is added; for the more sacred an oath appears to be, the more easily does an Arab violate it. But a convention concluded in this manner derives its force merely from opinion, and this is indeed extraordinary. . . . If a stranger who meets with them in the desert, or comes to a camp, or before he departs from a city, can oppose this alliance to their rapacity, his baggage and his life are more safe, even in the midst of the desert, than during the first days of his journey with the securities of twenty hostages. The Arab with whom he has eaten bread and salt, and all the Arabs of his tribe, consider him as their countryman and brother. There is no kind of respect, no proof of regard, which they do not show him."[1]

Volney says of the Druzes, "When they have contracted with their guests the sacred engagement of bread and salt, no subsequent event can make them violate it."[2] This Volney illustrates by notable incidents.

[1] Don Raphel's *The Bedouins, or Arabs of the Desert*, Part II, p. 59; quoted in Burder's *Oriental Customs*, 2d ed., p. 72 f.
[2] Volney's *Travels*, II., 76.

Mrs. Finn, wife of the English consul at Jerusalem, who was long resident in the East, gives the following illustration of the importance of salt as well as bread to a binding covenant. After a feast in the Hebron district of Palestine, one of the persons who shared it was waylaid and murdered by hired assassins. "One of the men (Abdallah) concerned in the deed, not as an actor, but as spectator, had been the night before actually eating with the victim. On hearing what had happened, the poor fellah woman who had cooked their supper, and who was much attached to the murdered man, bewailed herself, beating her breast and crying, 'Wo is me! wo is me! I left out the salt by mistake when making the bread last night for their supper. Oh that I had put it in! then would not Abdallah have dared to let my lord be murdered in his presence; he would have been compelled to defend him after eating his bread and salt. Wo is me! wo is me!'"[1]

John Macgregor, while on the upper Jordan in his canoe Rob Roy, was taken prisoner by the Arabs. As he parleyed with the old shaykh in his tent, Macgregor opened a box of fine salt and proffered a pinch of it to his captor. The shaykh had never before seen salt so white and fine, and, therefore, thinking it was

---

[1] *Survey of Western Palestine*, Special Papers, p. 355.

sugar, he tasted it. Instantly Macgregor put a portion also into his own mouth, and with a loud, laughing shout he clapped the old shaykh on his back.

The shaykh was dumbfounded. His followers wondered what had happened. "'What is it?' all asked from him. 'Is it sukker?' He answered demurely, 'La, meleh!' ("No, it's salt!") Even his home secretary laughed at his chief." "We had now eaten salt together," says Macgregor, "and in his own tent, and so he was bound by the strongest tie, and he knew it." The result was that Macgregor and his canoe were carried back in triumph to the river, and speeded on their way, while the people on the banks shouted "salaams" to their brother in the covenant of salt.[1]

Salt alone is a basis of an enduring covenant, but bread alone is not so. Yet bread and salt may be such a basis, because there is salt as well as bread there. So commonly does salt go with bread that it is the exception when they are not together. Our English Bible asks, at Job 6:6, "Can that which hath no savor be eaten without salt?" But the Septuagint reads: "Can bread be eaten without salt?"[2]

In India it is much the same as in Arabia, Palestine, and Persia. In the Mahabharata, the great

---
[1] Macgregor's *The Rob Roy on the Jordan*, p. 259 f.
[2] See Sweet's version of *The Septuagint*, in loco.

treasure-house of Hindoo wisdom, the covenant of bread and salt finds specific recognition. When Krishna urges the hero Karna to join with him in the war against the Kauravas, he says to him: "If you will accompany me and join the Pandavas, they will all respect you as their elder brother, and exalt you to the sovereignty." But Karna cannot be persuaded to this treacherous course, although he knows that to be true will cost him his life. "I have seen bad omens," he says, "and I know I shall be slain; but I have eaten the bread and salt of the Kauravas, and I am resolved to fight on their side."[1]

Again, when Yudhishthira asked permission of Bhishma and Drona to fight against the Kauravas, they granted his request, and at the same time said: "We fight on the side of the Kauravas because for many years we have eaten their bread and salt, or otherwise we would have fought for you."[2]

In Madagascar also the covenant of salt is known, as in other parts of the East.[3] And thus on every continent and on the islands of the sea.

---

[1] Wheeler's *History of India*, I., 271.
[2] *Ibid.*, I., 297 f. Compare this with Ezra 4 : 1-14.
[3] M. Hamelin's *Adventures in Madagascar*, quoted in "The Madagascar News," Sept. 9, 1893.

V
SALT REPRESENTING BLOOD

V

SALT REPRESENTING BLOOD

There are indications in the customs of primitive peoples that "blood" and "salt" are recognized as in some sense interchangeable in their natures, qualities, and uses. And in this, as in many another matter, the trend of modern science seems to be in the line of primitive indications.

Peoples who have not salt available are accustomed to substitute for it fresh blood, as though the essential properties of salt were obtainable in this way. An observant medical scientist, writing of his travels in eastern Equatorial Africa, tells of the habit of the Masai people of drinking the warm blood fresh from the bullocks they kill; and this he characterizes as "a wise though repulsive" proceeding, "as the blood thus drunk provided the salts so necessary in human economy; for the Masai do not partake of any salt in its common form."[1]

Similarly, Dr. David Livingstone noted the fact that

[1] Thomson's *Through Masai Land*, p. 430.

when he was among peoples who had difficulty in procuring salt, fresh-killed meat seemed to satisfy the natural craving for salt, while vegetable diet without salt caused indigestion.[1] In portions of China, also, where salt is not obtainable, or where it is too expensive for ordinary use, the blood of pigs or fowls is carefully preserved and eaten as if a substitute for salt.

Professor Bunge of Basel, who is quite an authority in the realm of physiological and pathological chemistry, speaking on the relation of salt and blood, says that "at every period, in every part of the world, and in every climate, there are people who use salt as well as those who do not. The people who take salt, though differing from each other in every other respect, are all characterized by a vegetable diet; in the same way, those who do not use any salt are all alike in taking animal food."

He says, moreover: "It is ... noteworthy that the people who live on an animal diet without salt, carefully avoid loss of blood when they slaughter the animals. This was told me by four different naturalists who have lived among flesh-eaters in various parts of northern Russia and Siberia. The Samoyedes, when dining off reindeer flesh, dip every mouthful in blood before eating it. The Esquimaux in Greenland

---

[1] Livingstone's *Travels in South Africa*, p. 26 f., 600.

are said to plug the wound as soon as they have killed a seal." Like testimony comes from India, Arabia, Africa, Australia, and various parts of America.[1]

The Jews of to-day, who are careful to drain the blood from slaughtered animals prepared for food, are accustomed to put salt freely on the meat thus drained. This is in accordance with the prescription of the Talmud, for the purpose of absorbing the blood not drawn out from the main bloodvessels. At the close of two hours from the slaughtering, the meat is washed for cooking. Whatever be the reason rendered for this application of salt, and its remaining on the flesh for a time, may there not thus be an instinctive supplying of the salts taken away by draining out the blood?

"Salt" and "salts" are terms often used interchangeably in the common mind. While they are distinct as employed by a scientist, it is not to be wondered at that they are confused by those who fail to note the differences; nor is it important to consider these differences in primitive thought and customs.

"A salt," as the chemists use the term, is a combination of an acid and a base. There are many salts in use in the world; among these the one best known

[1] Bunge's *Text-Book of Physiological and Pathological Chemistry*, Wooldridge's translation, pp. 122-129.

and most widely used and valued is sodium chloride, or what is popularly known as "common salt." This has been used and prized, the world over, among all classes of men, from the earliest historic times.

Salt has long been popularly claimed as an important element of the liquids of the body, as shown in the blood, in the tears, and in the perspiration, of mankind. Later scientific experiments have confirmed ancient and traditional claims, that saline injections avail like blood transfusion for the preservation of life in an emergency.[1]

It has long been common among ordinary people to administer salt to one taken with a hemorrhage of the lungs, or stomach, or nose. This is the folk-lore remedy in many regions. Moreover, under careful medical and surgical direction it is now customary in the hospitals to keep on hand a warm solution of salt to inject into the veins or tissues of persons brought in sinking from a sudden loss of blood. Whatever connection the two ideas—the popular and the scientific—may or may not have, it is not to be wondered at that it has long been thought that, when blood has gone out from the body, salt might well go in.

---

[1] See *Des Injections sous-cutanées massives de Solutions salines*, par le Dr. L. Fourmeaux, Paris, 1897, pp. 5-7 ; also Quain's *Dict. of Med.*, art. "Transf. of Salt."

Blood transfusion, by which the blood or life of a stronger or fresher person may permeate the being of a sinking one, has been known of for centuries, and there are at least traces of it in tradition from the earliest ages.[1] More recent experiments have shown that a saline solution is even safer and more efficacious than the warm blood from another life; now, therefore, this has largely taken the place of blood in supplying the waste occasioned by severe hemorrhages.[2] Various illustrations of this treatment are given as showing that when persons were in a very low condition through loss of blood, they have been rescued and restored through copious injections of a saline solution.[3]

The use of blood as food was forbidden to Noah and his sons after the Flood.[4] A tradition of the Turkish or Tatar nations says that Noah's son Japheth was their immediate ancestor, and that Toutug, or Toumuk, a grandson of Japheth, discovered salt as an article of diet by accidentally dropping a morsel of food on to salt earth, and thus becoming acquainted

---
[1] See *Blood Covenant*, pp. 115-126, with references to Pliny, and to Roussel, and others. See, also, Dr. Thomas G. Morton's *Transfusion of Blood;* W. H. Howell's *American Text Book of Physiology*, p. 362.

[2] See Dr. Bartholow's *Hypodermatic Medication*, pp. 126-142.

[3] See, for example, *Capital Operations without Anæsthesia and the Use of Large Saline Infusion in Acute Anæmia*, a paper read by Dr. Buchanan before the National Association of Railway Surgeons, pp. 18, 79.

[4] Gen. 9 : 4.

with the savor of salt.[1] This carries back the traditional discovery of salt to the age when blood was first forbidden as food.

It was long ago claimed by some that the red corpuscles of the blood are dependent for their color and vitality on the presence of salt, and recent scientific experiments and discussion have continued in the direction of the question thus raised.[2]

It has been shown by experiment that many of the lower animals, as well as man, are dependent for their life on salt in their blood. " When an animal is fed with a diet as far as possible free from salts, but otherwise sufficient, it dies of *salts-hunger*. The blood first loses inorganic material, then the organs. The total loss is very small in proportion to the quantity still retained in the body ; but it is sufficient to cause the death of a pigeon in three weeks, and of a dog in six, with marked symptoms of muscular and nervous weakness."[3] A mode of torture in former ages is said to have been to deprive a person of salt, and cause him to waste away with painful salt-hunger. It is said that this mode of torture is still employed in China.

An Armenian story says that when a band of their

---

[1] Price's *Mohammedan History*, II., 458.
[2] See W. H. Howell's *American Text Book of Physiology*, p. 334.
[3] Voit, cited in Stewart's *Manual of Physiology*, Baillière, Tindall, and Cox, 1895.

people was in a stronghold of the mountains, and was besieged by the Turks, the latter failing to subdue the former by other means cut off the supply of salt from the Armenians, and this quickly subdued them.

In 1830, a paper by Dr. W. Stevens, read before the London College of Physicians, and afterwards elaborated and published in a volume, contended that the salient ingredients of the blood, "the chief of which is common culinary salt, ... is the cause of the red color, of the fluidity, and of the stimulating property, of the vital current." Dr. Stevens claimed that the poison of the rattlesnake, and various other poisons, operate directly on the blood, and produce disease or death "by interfering with the agency of the saline matter."[1]

"On the subject of the poison of the rattlesnake," Dr. Stevens, in this work, asserts that "when the muriate of soda (common salt) is immediately applied to the wound, it is a complete antidote. 'When an Indian,' he says, 'is bitten by a snake, he applies a ligature above the part, and scarifies the wound to the very bottom; he then stuffs it with common salt, and after this it soon heals, without producing any effect on the general system.'" In view of the fact that it might be objected that the salt is not the essential means of cure, but is an addition to the cura-

[1] See London *Quarterly Review*, XLVIII., 96 (Dec., 1832, 375-391).

tive treatment, Dr. Stevens says that he has "seen a rabbit, that was under the influence of the rattlesnake poison, drink a saturated solution of muriate of soda with great avidity, and soon recover; while healthy rabbits would not taste one drop of the same strong saline water when it was put before them."

Dr. Stevens gives various illustrations, out of primitive customs, and in the experience of modern practitioners, of curative and prophylactic uses of salt in the treatment of fevers, where the condition of the blood seems to be a main source of evil. Aside from the question whether the claims of Dr. Stevens have been substantiated by later researches and experiments, his investigations and assertions are of interest as showing that, in the realm of modern science as of primitive practices, salt and blood have seemed to many to have interchangeable values.

If, indeed, this theory of Dr. Stevens, elaborated so carefully in the first third of the nineteenth century, in which he claims that salt practically represents blood, stood all by itself in the history of medicine, it would have less importance than it has in a formal treatise of this kind; yet even then it would show that such an idea had before now found a place in the human mind. But it by no means stands thus alone; a similar claim has been made both earlier and later.

Pliny, in his day, at the beginning of the Christian era, records it as the common belief that salt is foremost among human remedies for disease, and among preventives of sickness of all kinds.[1] He gives prominence to salt as a cure of leprosy,[2] whereas blood transfusion and blood bathing was the traditional treatment of that disorder.[3] Pliny also speaks of salt itself, and of salt fish in large quantities, as a supposed remedy for the bite of serpents,[4] this being in the line of asserted remedies among the Indians, according to Dr. Stevens. Various other disorders, especially of the blood, are named by Pliny as curable by salt.

Seventy years after the treatise of Dr. Stevens, a volume, recently published in London by C. Godfrey Gümpel on "Common Salt,"[5] claims even more than Pliny, or any writer since his day, for "the vital importance of common salt for our whole physical and social life." He claims that of all the constituents of our life's blood "there is none which can possibly surpass common salt in its necessity for a strong healthy blood,"[6] and that both the red corpuscles and the white are largely dependent for their normal condition on "the presence of common salt in the system."[7]

[1] *Hist. Nat.*, XXXI., 45.   [2] *Ibid.*
[3] *Blood Covenant*, pp. 116 f., 125, 287 f., 324.
[4] *Hist. Nat.*, XXXI., 41; XXXII., 17.
[5] *Common Salt: Its Use and Necessity for the Maintenance of Health and the Prevention of Disease*, p. 1.   [6] *Ibid.*, p. 37.   [7] *Ibid.*, p. 41.

A writer in the Asiatic Quarterly Review, not long ago declared that the government salt monopoly of the British Empire in India (since practically abolished, or modified) was a cause of greater evils than those resulting from either opium or alcohol. This claim is based on the idea that a lack of salt by the common people of India tends to a deterioration of blood and consequent loss of life. Asiatic cholera is said to be promoted by the lack of salt in the blood. Men and cattle alike are said to be sufferers from this cause, and the soil is rendered less fertile. Whether this idea is well grounded is a minor matter; that the idea has been in many minds is not to be questioned.

Thus it will be seen that in the primitive mind salt and blood have seemed to have common properties, and to be in a sense interchangeable, while the more careful observers in the world of science have rather grown toward this thought than away from it. Be it correct or incorrect, the human mind has never been able to rid itself of the idea.

Salt is sometimes used in the rite of blood brotherhood among primitive peoples, as is also wine, both wine and salt being counted the equivalent of blood, and the original and the substitute being sometimes employed together as if to intensify the symbolism. Stanley tells of the use of salt in this rite on the occasion of its performance with Ngalyema in the Congo region.¹ And so again in other cases.²

It is a common practice in the East to welcome an honored guest to one's house by sacrificing an animal at the doorway, and letting its blood pour out on the threshold, to be stepped over by the guest, as a mode of adoption, or of covenant-making.³ When such a guest comes unexpectedly, and there is not time to obtain an animal for the welcoming sacrifice, it is customary to take salt and strew it in lieu of blood on the threshold,—salt being thus recognized as the equivalent, or as a representative, of blood.⁴

The measure of love and honor accorded to the welcomed guest is indicated by the cost or preciousness of the sacrifice on the threshold. There are traditions, at least, of the sacrifice of a son of the host in this way. Again a favorite horse has been thus sacrificed. More frequently it is a lamb that is the sacrifice. If there is no lamb available, a fowl or a pigeon is thus offered. The essential factor in every case is the blood, the life, outpoured. If, however, no actual blood is obtainable, salt, as representing blood, is accepted as indicating the love and the spirit which prompts the

¹ *The Congo*, I., 383-385. ² *Ibid.*, II., 21-24, 79-90.
³ See *Threshold Covenant*, passim.
⁴ *Ibid.*, p. 5 ; Griffis's *Mikado's Empire*, pp. 467, 470 ; Isabella Bird's *Untrodden Tracks in Japan*, I., 392.

welcome, according to the giver's means. There could hardly be a fuller proof of the identity of salt and blood in the primitive mind.

When a Siamese student was asked by the writer whether the rite of blood-covenanting was known in his land, he replied: "There is no 'blood covenant' so far as I know. The custom is, if two persons are desirous to become firm friends or brothers they drink together *salted water;* then each takes an oath." He also suggested that he had heard that in former times they drank *a fowl's blood* in this rite.

Again, the mode of making a covenant of salt in some portions of the East coincides with this suggested identification of salt with blood in the primitive mind. In the Lebanon region, where the blood covenant, as a bond of union, is still recognized and practised,[1] the covenant of salt is also well known, not only as between new comers who are to enter into a mutual alliance, but as bringing into union friends who would be as one. In such cases a sword is taken, and salt is laid on its blade. The two friends in turn lick of the salt that is to unite them, as if they were tasting of common blood after the fashion of the "blood-lickers" in Mecca.[2]

[1] See *Blood Covenant*, pp. 5-7.
[2] See Smith's *Kinship and Marriage in Early Arabia*, p. 48.

Another illustration of this mode is given by Sir Frederick Henniker, in his notes of a journey in the East in 1819-20.[1] It was a shaykh of the Arabs who escorted him from Mt. Sinai northward, who cut this covenant with Sir Frederick. On the request being made for such an assurance of fidelity from the shaykh, "he immediately drew his sword," says Sir Frederick, "placed some salt upon the blade, and then put a portion of it into his mouth, and desired me to do the same; and 'Now, cousin,' said he, 'your life is as sacred as my own;' or, as he expressed himself, 'Son of my uncle, your head is upon my shoulders.'" Before this act the two were as cousins; now they were as one, the head of one being upon the shoulders of the other. The similarity of this rite with that of the blood covenant, in both its form and meaning, is obvious.

This correspondence of salt and blood in primitive thought, and in fact, will perhaps throw light on a disputed reference in a fragment of Ennius[2] to "*salsus sanguis*" (salted blood, or briny blood). It would seem that as the Jews held that the blood is the life, and the life is in the blood, similarly Greeks and Romans recognized the truth that salt is in the blood, and the blood is salt.

[1] *Visit to Egypt, Nubia*, etc., p. 242.   [2] Cited in *Macrobius*, 6, 2.

In the second century there were Christian ascetics who refused to take wine in the eucharist. Among these the Elkesaites and the Ebionites employed bread and salt instead of bread and wine. This seems to have been a recognition of the fact that salt, like wine, represented blood.[1]

Professor Hermann Collitz, of Bryn Mawr, has suggested, in this connection, that the very words, in Latin, for salt and blood, *sal* and *sanguis*, are from the same root.[2]

Certainly salt is sometimes used as a substitute for blood in primitive covenanting; on the other hand, blood is used for salt among some primitive peoples as an essential accompaniment of food. These facts being noticed by the author of this volume first suggested to him the real meaning of the covenant of salt.

[1] See Clementine, *Homilies*, IV. 6; XIII. 8; XIV. 1, 8; XIX. 25, cited in art. "Elkesai" in Smith and Wace's *Dict. of Christian Biog.*

[2] Professor Collitz says, on this point: "The Early European word for salt, *sal* (nominative *sāl-d*, genitive *sal-n-és* according to Joh. Schmidt) which probably goes back to the Indo-European period, may be derived from the same root to which the Sanskrit *ás-r-g* (genitive *as-n-ás*) 'blood,' and Latin *s-an-gu-i-s* (genitive *s-an-gu-in-is*) belong. The latter, as F. de Saussure (*Système primitif des voyelles Indo-Européennes*, Leipzig, 1897, p. 225) has shown, comes from a root *es*, which lost its initial vowel if the suffix was accented. If we connect the two groups of words, we should say that *sal* is derived from this root *es* by a suffix *al*, similar to the suffix *el* in the word for 'sum' (Indo-European *sā'v-el*, from root *sāv*), or to the suffix *a-lo* in Greek *meg-a-lo-s* as compared with *meg-a-s*. The root *es* is probably the same from which the word for 'to be' (Sanskrit *as-mi*, Latin *sum*) is derived, and the meaning of which seems to have been originally 'to live.'"

VI
SALT REPRESENTING LIFE

VI

SALT REPRESENTING LIFE

As blood is synonymous with life in primitive thought and practice,[1] and as salt has been shown to represent blood in the primitive mind, so salt seems to stand for life in many a form of primitive speech and in the world's symbolism. When, indeed, we speak of salt as preserving flesh from corruption, we refer to the staying of the process of death by an added element of life ; preserving by re-vivifying, rather than by embalming.

Plutarch says of the power of salt in this direction : "All flesh is dead and part of a lifeless carcass ; but the virtue of salt being added to it, like a soul, gives it a pleasing relish and poignancy."[2] All life is from the one Source of Life, and in this sense it is that life is divine. Thus Plutarch calls attention to the fact that Homer[3] speaks of salt as "divine," and that " Plato delivers, that by man's laws salt is to be ac-

[1] See *Blood Covenant*, passim.
[2] Plutarch's *Symposiacs* (Goodwin's ed.), Book IV., Quest. IV., § 3.
[3] Homer's *Iliad*, IX., 214.

counted most sacred."¹ No other material is thus reckoned from primitive days sacred and divine, unless it be blood, which is the synonym of life.²

An Oriental form of oath sometimes substitutes "salt" for "life;" as where the prime minister of Persia in a conference with James Morier, secretary of the English embassy, at Teheran, early in this century, swore "by the salt of Fatti Ali Shah"—the then reigning Shah of Persia.³ Indeed, to swear "by the salt" is a common form of asseveration among Arabs; as to swear by the life, one's own or another's, is a well-known oath in the East.⁴

Where we would say of one who is foremost in inspiriting and enlivening a social gathering, "He was the *life* of the party," the Arabs say, "He was the *salt* of the party."

The "salt of youth" is synonymous with the virility and vigor of life, that show themselves in the age of strong passion. Thus Justice Shallow says to Master Page : " Though we are justices and doctors and churchmen, Master Page, we have some salt of

---

¹ Plutarch's *Symposiacs* (Goodwin's ed.), Book V., Quest. X., §§ 1, 2.

² Lev. 17 : 11 ; Deut. 12 : 23. *Blood Covenant*, p. 38 f.

³ Morier's *Journey through Persia*, p. 200.

⁴ See, for example, Arvieux on *Customs of Bedouin Arabs*, p. 43, quoted in Rosenmüller's *Das alte und des neue Morgenland*, II., 15.

our youth in us."[1] Iago refers to young gallants in their passion, "as salt as wolves in pride."[2] And Menecrates refers to "salt Cleopatra" in her loves with Antony.[3] Mrs. Browning seems to have a similar idea as to the significance of salt, when she says in "A Vision of Poets:"

> "And poor, proud Byron,—sad as grave
> And salt as life; forlornly brave,
> And quivering with the dart he drave."

Even in Plutarch's day this truth was recognized by the Greeks as possibly having influenced the ancient Egyptians to forbid salt to their priests, who must be pure and chaste, because salt "by its heat is provocative and apt to raise lust."[4] It would seem, however, that the prohibition of salt as food to Egyptian priests is easier to be accounted for by the fact that it was recognized as the equivalent of blood and life. Therefore those priests were not to partake of salt, "no, not so much as in their bread."[5]

In this line of thought Florus says of salt: "Consider farther whether its power of preserving a long time dead bodies from rotting be not a *divine*

---
[1] *Merry Wives of Windsor*, Act II., Scene 3.
[2] *Othello*, Act III., Scene 3.
[3] *Antony and Cleopatra*, Act II., Scene 1.
[4] Plutarch's *Symposiacs*, Book V., Quest. X., §§ 1, 2.   [5] *Ibid.*

property, and opposite to death; since it preserves part, and will not suffer that which is mortal wholly to be destroyed. But as the soul, which is our diviner part, connects the limbs of animals, and keeps the composure from dissolution; thus salt applied to dead bodies, and imitating the work of the soul, stops those parts that were falling to corruption, binds and confines them, and so makes them keep their union and agreement with one another." [1]

Philinus goes a step farther when he asks: "Do you not think that that which is generative is to be esteemed divine, seeing God is the principle of all things?" [2] And Plutarch adds suggestively that salt is by some supposed to be a means of life, not only exciting desire for generation, but actually causing procreation; "the females (among the lower animals), as some imagine, conceiving without the help of the males, only by licking salt. But [as he thinks] it is most probable that the salt raiseth an itching in animals, and so makes them salacious and eager to couple. And perhaps for the same reason they call a surprising and bewitching beauty, such as is apt to move and entice, *halmuron kai drimu*, 'saltish.' And I think the poets had a respect to this genera-

---

[1] Plutarch's *Symposiacs*, Book V., Quest. X., §§ 1, 2.   [2] *Ibid.*

tive power of salt in their fable of Venus springing from the sea."[1]

In Central and South America it was deemed necessary to abstain from salt while praying and sacrificing, with a desire to obtain children. So far it was among the Maya nations of the New World as among the priests of Ancient Egypt.[2]

An Oriental proverb says : "If thou takest the salt [the life, or soul] from the flesh [the body] then thou mayest throw it [the flesh] to the dogs." This has been explained by the rabbis, as considering "salt" here synonymous with the soul, or life, of man, which comes from God, in distinction from man's body, which comes from his parents. "God gives the spirit [the breath], the soul, the features, the hearing, the organs of speech, the gait, the perceptions, the reason, and the intuition. When now the time comes for man to depart out of the world, God takes his part, and the part which comes from the parents [the body] he lays before them."[3]

When Elisha, the prophet of Israel, was met by the men of Jericho, as he came from the scene of Elijah's translation to enter upon his mission as the

---

[1] Plutarch's *Symposiacs*, Book V., Quest. X., §§ 1, 2.
[2] See Bancroft's *Native Races of the Pacific Coast*, II., 678.
[3] Niddah 31 a, quoted by Rev. Dr. Marcus Jastrow in *The Sunday School Times* for April 28, 1894.

successor of Elijah and was told of the death-dealing power of the waters of the city, his words and action seemed to emphasize the correspondence of salt with life. " He said, Bring me a new cruse, and put salt therein. And they brought it to him. And he went forth unto the spring of the waters, and cast salt therein, and said, Thus saith the Lord, I have healed these waters; there shall not be from thence any more death or miscarrying [of the land]. So the waters were healed [were restored to life] unto this day, according to the word of Elisha which he spake." [1]

A spring of water is in itself so important to a primitive people that it is not to be wondered at that water is called the Gift of God, and that a living spring is looked at as in a sense divine, and that it has even been worshiped as a god among primitive peoples.[2] When, therefore, salt, as the synonym of life or of blood, is found in a spring of living water, it is natural to recognize the spot as peculiarly favored of God, or of the gods. Thus "among inland peoples a salt spring was regarded as a special gift of the gods. The Chaonians in Epirus had one which flowed into a stream where there were [as in the Dead Sea] no fish; and the legend was that Heracles had allowed their

---

[1] 2 Kings 2 : 19-22.
[2] See *Kadesh-barnea*, p. 36, and note, 298 f.; and *Studies in Oriental Social Life*, pp. 213, 404 f.

forefathers to have salt instead of fish (*Aristotle*). The Germans waged war for saline streams, and believed that the presence of salt invested a district with peculiar sanctity, and made it a place where prayers were most readily heard (Tacitus, *Ann.*, XIII., 57)." [1]

There is said to be a salt lake in the mountain region of Koordistan, which was changed from fresh water to salt, by St. Peter, when he first came thither preaching Christianity. He wrought this change so that he could influence the people to accept his teaching through sharing his life by partaking of the salt. To this day the tradition remains, that, if the natives will bathe in that lake, they will renew their faith. Aside from the question of any basis of truth in the legend, it remains as a survival of the primitive idea of a real connection of shared salt with shared life.

It is customary among some primitive peoples to anoint or smear a new-born babe with blood, as a means of giving him more and fuller life.[2] Thus among the ancient Caribs, of South America, "as soon as a male child was brought into the world, he was sprinkled with some drops of his father's blood;" the father "fondly believing that the same degree of courage which he had himself displayed, was by these

---

[1] W. Robertson Smith in art. "Salt" in *Encyc. Brit.*, 9th ed.
[2] *Blood Covenant*, p. 137 f.

means transmitted to his son."[1] In one of the Kaffir tribes of South Africa, when a new chief assumes authority, it was customary to wash him in the blood of a near relative, generally a brother, who was put to death on the occasion. In order to give more life and character to the freshly elevated representative of the ruling family, the family life was drawn from the veins of one near him, in order that it might be absorbed by him who could use it more imposingly.[2]

The Bheels are a brave and warlike race of mountaineers of Hindostan. They claim to have been, formerly, the rulers of all their region, but either by defeat in war or by voluntary concession to have yielded their power to other peoples, whom they now authorize to rule in their old domain. When, therefore, a new rajput, or chief ruler, comes into power in any of the surrounding countries, this right to rule is conceded, or ratified, by an anointing of blood drawn from the toe or thumb of a Bheel. The right of giving this blood, or new life, is claimed by particular Bheel families; and the belief that the individual from whose veins the blood is drawn never lives beyond a twelvemonth, in no degree operates to repress the desire of the Bheels to furnish the blood of anointing.[3]

---

[1] Edwards's *Hist. of Brit. West Ind.*, I. 47, referred to in *Blood Covenant*, p. 137 f. [2] Shooter's *Kafirs of Natal*, p. 216, *ibid*. [3] *Trans. Royal Asiat. Soc.*, I., 69, *ibid*.

Salt is similarly used to-day, in the East and elsewhere.[1] A new-born child is at once washed and salted. If an Oriental seems lacking in life or wisdom, or is, as we would say, exceptionally "fresh," it is said of him, "He wasn't salted when he was born." This idea would seem to be included in the prophet's reproach of Jerusalem: "Neither wast thou washed in water to cleanse thee; thou wast not salted at all, nor swaddled at all."[2]

As at birth, so at death, salt seems to stand in primitive thought for blood, or life, in washing or anointing, in the hope of supplying the special lack or need of the individual. Among the cannibals of Borneo, on the death of a rajah or chief, the desire seems to be to restore him to life if it be possible. His body is rubbed or bathed with salt. He is then dressed in his best apparel, and placed in a sitting posture. In his hands are placed his shield and mandau. If this application of new life and this special appeal to action fail to arouse him, he is counted as hopelessly dead; the arms are taken from him, the body is undressed, and wrapped in a piece of cloth, and placed in the ground.[3]

A traveler in Asia Minor speaks of the practice

---
[1] Van Lennep's *Bible Lands*, p. 569.   [2] Ezek. 16 : 4.
[3] Carl Bock's *Head Hunters of Borneo*, p. 224.

among the Toorkomans of the mother's dipping a child two or three times into a skin of salt water, at the time of his naming. This would seem to be a primitive rite, and not a Christian one. The father of the child meanwhile eats honeyed cake, and drinks thickened milk.[1]

Milk is sometimes accepted by the Arabs as a substitute for salt, as the essential factor in the covenant of salt (the *milḥa*).[2] Milk is nature's life food, it stands for liquid life; two "milk brothers" are somewhat as blood brothers, brothers by a common life.[3] "There seem to be indications," says W. Robertson Smith,[4] "that many primitive peoples regard milk as a kind of equivalent for blood as containing a sacred life. Thus to eat a kid seethed in its mother's milk might be taken as an equivalent to eating 'with the blood,' and be forbidden to the Hebrews[5] along with the bloody sacraments of the heathen."

Milk has been employed instead of blood, and again of salt, for transfusion in case of declining life from hemorrhage.[6] This would seem to justify the

---

[1] W. Eassie, in *Notes and Queries*, 3d series, II., 318.
[2] See references, in W. Robertson Smith's *Religion of the Semites* (p. 252, note), to Burckhardt and to *Kâmil*.
[3] *Blood Covenant*, pp. 10, 11.
[4] *Relig. of the Sem.*, p. 204, note; also *Kinship and Marriage in Early Arabia*, pp. 149, 150.   [5] Exod. 23 : 19 ; 34 : 26 ; Deut. 14 : 21.
[6] Quain's *Dict. of Medicine*, art. "Transfusion of Milk."

belief that milk and blood alike represent life in popular thought.

A favorite experiment among young folks is to bring life to dead flies by covering them with salt. When flies are drowned purposely, or by accident, if one is taken from the water apparently dead, and laid on the table, or on a plate, and covered with common salt, in a few seconds the fly will creep out from under the salt, and soon fly away as if unharmed. Other flies in the same condition, not treated with salt, remain as dead. This has been tried by succeeding generations of young folks, and it is one of the folk-lore facts in support of the idea that salt is life.

It may, of course, be that the absorbent power of salt clears the trachea of the fly, and thus permits the restoration of the natural breathing. Of course, there is some explanation of the phenomenon; but the fact remains that the common mind has been affected by such things in the direction of the belief that salt is life in a peculiar sense.

After the foregoing pages were already in type, it was cabled as news from London that an English mechanic claimed to have discovered a method of resuscitating persons who have been drowned. He proposed to cover the entire body of the person taken from the water with dry salt, which is supposed to absorb the moisture, and thus draw the water from the lungs and permit the air again to circulate freely. He claimed to have revived a recently drowned cat, after letting it remain under salt for thirty minutes; and that a drowned dog was thus restored in two hours.

This is simply the folk-lore idea of bringing the dead to life by the application of salt as life. Like many another folk-lore idea, it is deserving of attention because of some possible basis of truth below the idea, apart from the question of fact in connection with the claim.

In "The Barber's Story of his Fifth Brother," in "The Arabian Nights," is an account of the hero's being beaten and slashed until he was supposed to be dead from loss of blood, and his other injuries. Then a slave-girl, named El-Meleehah, the "salt-bearer," came and stuffed salt into his gaping wounds, after which his supposed corpse was thrown into a subterranean vault among the dead. Yet by means of this application of salt he was saved to life, and regained his pristine vigor.[1]

The references of Jesus to salt would seem to have fuller meaning, if "salt" be understood as equivalent to "life." Where he says to his disciples: "Ye are the salt of the earth: but if the salt have lost its savor,

[1] Lane's *Thousand and One Nights*, I, 365.

wherewith shall it be salted? it is thenceforth good for nothing, but to be cast out and trodden under foot of men,"[1] he would seem to remind them that they are the life of the world, if, indeed, they retain life in themselves. And where he says, "Have salt in yourselves, and be at peace one with another,"[2] he would call them to have life in themselves, and to join with others who have it, in making their life to be felt among their fellows.

A supposed utterance of Jesus, which has been a puzzle to critics and commentators, possibly has light thrown on it in this view of salt as corresponding with life. Discoursing on life, and the wisdom of striving to attain or to enter into life, even at a loss of much that man might value here on earth, Jesus, according to some manuscripts, said, "For every one shall be salted with fire."[3] This sentence is disputed by some, not being found in all the more ancient MSS., and its meaning does not seem to be clear to any.[4] It is obvious that whatever else "salted" here means, it does not mean "salted." To salt is to mingle, or to accompany, with salt. Clearly, fire does not do that. The Greek is as vague, or as ambiguous, as the English.

---

[1] Matt. 5: 13; Luke 14: 34.   [2] Mark 9: 50.
[3] Mark 9: 49. Comp. A. V. and R. V.
[4] See notes and references in Nicoll's *Expositors' Greek Testament;* Lange's *Commentary;* Meyer's *Commentary*, in loco, etc.

There must be a conventional or popular, a figurative or symbolical, meaning in which "salt" is here used. What can this be?

"Fire" is here spoken of as the synonym, or equivalent, or parallel, of "salt." In this figure, *fire* is to accomplish what *salt* performs; the work of *salt* is to be done by *fire*. In what sense can this be true? Fire does consume and destroy the perishable;[1] it does bring out and refine that which is permanent and precious;[2] it does try and test and reveal the measure of real value in that which is submitted to it.[3] In the testing time, "each man's work shall be made manifest: for the day shall declare it, because it is revealed in fire; and the fire itself shall prove each man's work, of what sort it is. If any man's work shall abide which he built thereon [on the one Foundation], he shall receive a reward. If any man's work shall be burned he shall suffer loss: but he himself [who has builded] shall be saved; yet as through fire."[4]

The whole context of the passage in Mark's Gospel indicates that Jesus is speaking of *life*. He is showing the way to attain to life. He points to the final testing of life by fire. As salt is shown to correspond with life, and as this seems to have been understood

---

[1] Gen. 19 : 24, 25; Exod. 9 : 23, 24; Lev. 10 : 2; 13 : 52-57; Matt. 3 : 12; 7 : 19; Luke 3 : 17; John 15 : 6.
[2] Mal. 3 : 2, 3.   [3] 1 Pet. 1 : 7.   [4] 1 Cor. 3 : 13-15.

by his hearers, would they not have seen that Jesus was pointing out that the measure of life, or salt, the reminder of God's covenant with his people, in every one of them, would be revealed in the testing of fire?

It is, indeed, because salt represents life, that salt was to accompany every sacrifice under the Jewish dispensation. Not death, but life, was an acceptable offering to God, according to the teachings of the Bible, both in the Old Testament and the New.[1] God wants "not yours, but you."[2] This was emphasized by priest and prophet in the history of the Jewish people, earlier and later. Paul re-echoed this primal thought when he appealed to Christians: "I beseech you therefore, brethren, by the mercies of God, to present your bodies ⌊yourselves⌋ a *living* sacrifice, holy, acceptable to God, which is your reasonable service."[3] Without salt, without the symbol of life, no sacrifice was to be counted a fitting or acceptable offering at God's altar.

Salt is taken, in the world's thought, as an equivalent of wit, or lively wisdom, in speech. Thus Paul counsels the Colossian Christians: "Let your speech be always with grace, seasoned with salt, that ye may know how ye ought to answer each one."[4] Because

---

[1] See *Blood Covenant*, passim.
[2] 2 Cor. 12 : 14. [3] Rom. 12 : 1. [4] Col. 4 : 6.

the Athenians were noted for their life and wit in speech, "Attic salt" was a synonym of truest life in conversation. Cicero says of Scipio: "*Scipio omnes sale superbat*" ("Scipio surpassed all in salt," or "wit").

Pliny after describing the properties and uses of salt, says: "We may conclude then, by Hercules! that the higher enjoyments of life could not exist without the use of salt: indeed, so highly necessary is this substance to mankind, that the pleasures of the mind, even, can be expressed by no better term than the word 'salt,' such being the name given to all effusions of wit. All the amenities, in fact, of life, supreme liberty, and relaxation from toil [in a word, 'life,'] can find no word in our language to characterize them better than this."[1]

Pliny also calls attention to the fact that "salarium," from which we derive our word "salary," was the "salt money," bestowed as a reward or honorarium on successful generals and military tribunes.[2] The idea of a "living," or a support of life, is in the word "salary." And so when we say that a man is "not worth his salt," we mean that he is not worth his living.

Salt has been employed as money at various times

[1] *Hist. Nat.*, XXXI., 41.   [2] *Ibid.*

and in various lands, and thus has been the means of supporting life. It has been so in Tibet and in India, and in the heart of Africa along from the sixth to the nineteenth centuries of our era. Thus even in lands where gold is abundant but less valued than salt.[1]

It is said of the people of a province in Tibet, that, while they reckon the value of gold by weight, the nearest approach to coined money which they have is in molded and stamped cakes of salt. "On this money ... the Prince's mark is printed; and no one is allowed to make it except the royal officers. ... Merchants take this currency and go to those tribes that dwell among the mountains; ... and there they get a *saggio* of gold for sixty, or fifty, or forty pieces of this salt money; ... for in such positions they cannot dispose at pleasure of their gold and other things, such as musk and the like; ... and so they give them cheap." "This exchange of salt-cakes for gold, forms a curious parallel to the like exchange in the heart of Africa, narrated by Cosmas in the sixth century, and by Aloisio Cadamosto in the fifteenth."[2]

Victor Hehn calls attention to the fact that "the German copper-coin heller (haller or häller), the smallest coin still in use in Austria, referred to in

---

[1] Marco Polo's *Travels*, Col. Yule's translation, II., 29, 35, 36, 37, and notes to Chap. 47.   [2] *Ibid.*

the German saying, 'to have not a red heller,' derives its name from the salt (*hal*), and the place where it was obtained."[1]

Pythagoras, speaking as usual in figurative terms, described salt as a preserver of all things, as continuing life and as staying corruption, or death. He directed the keeping of a vessel of salt on every table, as a reminder of its essential qualities.[2]

Pliny says, moreover, that there are mountains of salt in different countries in India, from which great blocks are cut as from a quarry; and that from this source a larger revenue is secured by the rulers than from all their gold and pearls.[3]

In many countries of the world salt is a matter of government control, its manufacture and disposition being guarded as if life and death were involved in it. It is a common saying in Italy that a man must not dip up a bucket of water from the Mediterranean Sea; for he might make salt from the water, and so defraud the government.

[1] Victor Hehn's *Das Salz*, p. 72.
[2] See Dacier's *Life of Pythagoras* (Eng. trans.), pp. 60, 105.
[3] *Hist. Nat.*, XXXI., 39.

VII
SALT AND SUN, LIFE AND LIGHT

VII

SALT AND SUN, LIFE AND LIGHT

In Oriental and primitive thought Salt and Sun are closely connected, even if they are not considered as identical. They stand together as Life and Light. Their mention side by side in various places tends to confirm this view of their remarkable correspondence. The similarity of their forms accords with the Oriental delight in a play upon words, even apart from the question of any similarity in their meanings.

Pliny, who, while not an original thinker, was a faithful and industrious collater of the sayings and doings of his contemporaries, and those who had gone before him, especially in the realm of material things, summed up the popular beliefs as to salt and its uses in the declaration that there is nothing better for the human body, in health or in sickness, than salt and sun, "*sale et sole.*" [1]

Not only in the English and the Latin, but in the Greek, the Kymric, and the Keltic, this similarity in

---

[1] *Hist. Nat.*, XXXI., 45.

the form of the words for salt and sun is to be observed. The Greek *hals* and *helios*, the Welsh *hal* and *haul*, the Irish *sal* and *sul*, illustrate this so far as the form is concerned.[1] As to the signification of the words, it has already been shown that "salt" represents "life" in primitive thought and speech. Similarly the sun was considered "as the life-giver, the emblem of procreation." In consequence, "son" and "sun" are from the same root.[2] In view of this it is not strange that salt and sun, as life and light, were considered in primitive and popular thought as the means of health and hope for mankind.

"The root of the word for salt is unknown. The name of the sun is apparently a derivation from the root *su* (or *sāv*) 1. To generate. 2. To impel, to set in motion, to bring about."[3] If the same be not the root of the word "salt," there is at least reason for thinking that the meaning of the two words "salt" and "sun" are similar,—one gives life, the other represents life.

To the primitive mind it certainly would seem natural to ascribe the creation of salt to the action or

---

[1] In the Old Irish and the Old Welsh *s* and *h* interchange, as they do in the Zend. See Table of Grimm, in Sayce's *Introduction to the Science of Language*, I., 305.

[2] Skeat's *Etymological Dictionary*, at words "Salt," "Son," "Solar," "Sun;" also Kluge's *Etymological Dictionary*, s. v. "*Sonne*."

[3] According to Prof. Dr. Hermann Collitz, of Bryn Mawr. Compare Joh. Schmidt in Kuhn's "Zeitschrift," XXVI., 9; and O. Schrader, *Prehistoric Antiquities of the Aryan Peoples*, p. 414. Trans. by F. B. Jevons.

power of the sun. Peculiarly would this be the case with dwellers by the ocean or sea, or inland salt lakes. As the sun shines upon the water drawn from the sea or lake, the water is evaporated and the salt remains. This is the ordinary process of salt-making with all its benefits in various countries to the present day. What thought is more natural, in view of this recognized fact, than that the sun is the generator, or the begetter, of salt which is life? If the sun is supposed to bring life, in what way does it more directly accomplish this than by this salt creation?

This would seem to give added significance and force to the words of Jesus as to salt and light. If in the days of Jesus it was held, as Pliny says, that there was nothing that could help the life of humanity like salt and sun, life and light, the disciples of Jesus must have recognized a peculiar meaning in the teachings of the Great Physician as he sent them out into the world to heal the sick, and raise the dead, and cleanse the lepers, and cast out demons,[1] when he suggested that it was what they were, rather than what they did, that was to be the help of humanity. In the same teaching he said, "Ye are the salt of the earth," "Ye are the light of the world."[2]

The recognized meaning of these words in the days

[1] Matt. 10 : 8.   [2] Matt. 5 : 13, 14.

of Jesus intensified their importance at every use of them, as when it was said that "in Him was life; and the life was the light of men."[1] Salt was blood; blood was life; salt was life; life was light; blood and salt and light were life.

Among folk-lore customs on both sides of the ocean, salt and a candle are carried across the threshold on moving to a new house, as if representing life and light as needs in a new home. Sometimes the Bible also is included, as if in recognition of the true basis of all sacred covenanting. There are other folk-lore customs connecting salt and light.[2]

According to Professor Dr. Hilprecht, in the old Assyrian language, *ṭâbtu*, "salt," and *ṭâbtu*, "blessing," have the same ideogram, and are written exactly alike. "This suggests the inquiry whether they are not derived from the same root, *ṭâbu*, 'to be good,' and whether *ṭâbtu*, 'salt,' was not so called by the Assyrians as the great blessing given to man, as needed more than aught else for the preparation of food and the preservation of life."

[1] John 1 : 4.   [2] See Chap. X., *infra*.

VIII

SIGNIFICANCE OF BREAD

VIII

SIGNIFICANCE OF BREAD

Bread is the basis of a common meal, as blood is the basis of a common life. As, in the sacrifices, the body of the animal offered in sacrifice was the basis of a covenant meal, while the blood was the basis of union with the divine; so in the symbolism of bread and wine, in any sacramental meal, or in any meal of sacred covenanting between two persons, the bread stood for the flesh, and the wine for the blood. So, also, when bread and salt are used together, the salt would seem to stand for blood or life, and the bread to stand for the flesh or the body.[1]

Blood gives life; flesh as food gives sustenance. Salt represents life; bread represents sustaining food. In this light those who share salt together are in a life-sharing covenant; those who share bread together are sharers in a common growth. Covenant union in

[1] See *Blood Covenant*, pp. 182-190; 268 f.; 350-355.

sacrifice is secured or consummated by blood-sharing; it is evidenced or celebrated by food-sharing.

"Milk and honey" seem to be a symbol of blood and flesh, or of salt and bread, from a divine source. They are supplied to man from the vegetable world, through the agency of living animals, by the power of the Author of life. They stand for the vivifying and nourishing of the body by a providential ministry to man. In this light they seem to be viewed by primitive peoples. The Land of Promise was represented to the ancient Hebrews as "a land flowing with milk and honey,"[1] and this figure seemed to represent to them all that could be desired in the line of God's ministry to their material needs. It was many times repeated to them, or by them, in this sense.[2]

This symbolism was preserved by the early Christians in connection with the rite of baptism. Tertullian describing that rite says: "Having come out from the bath, we are anointed with a blessed unction of holy oil;" afterwards "we first taste a mixture of honey and milk."[3]

---

[1] Exod. 3 : 8, 17; 13 : 5; 33 : 3.

[2] Lev. 20 : 24; Num. 13 : 27; 14 : 8; 16: 13, 14; Deut. 6 : 3; 11 : 9; 26 : 9, 15; 27 : 3; 31 : 20; Josh. 5 : 6; Jer. 11 : 5; 32 : 22; Ezek. 20 : 6, 15.

[3] Tertullian. *De Coron.*, v. 3, *adv. Prox.* XXVI., *de Bapt.* vii. and viii., cited in Blunt's *Annotated Book of Common Prayer*, p. 209.

IX

SALT IN SACRIFICES

IX

SALT IN SACRIFICES

Salt seems to have been recognized as a vital element in sacrifices both in the teachings of the Bible and in the customs of the pagan world. In the Lord's injunction to Israel, it is said unqualifiedly: "And every oblation of thy meal offering shalt thou season with salt; neither shalt thou suffer the salt of the covenant of thy God to be lacking from thy meal offering: with all thine oblations [offerings bloody or unbloody] thou shalt offer salt."[1]

An alternative reading of the words of Jesus in Mark's Gospel refers to this custom when it says that "every sacrifice shall be salted with salt."[2] Josephus, in his "Antiquities of the Jews," makes reference to the large quantities of salt required for sacrifices.[3] This corresponds with the provision of the King of Persia for Jewish sacrifices, "salt without prescribing how much,"[4]—a limitless or indefinite amount.

[1] Lev. 2 : 13. See also Ezek. 43 : 21-24.
[2] Mark 9 : 49. These words are by some critics counted a gloss; yet the fact as a fact, with reference to salt in sacrifices, is undisputed.
[3] *Antiquities of the Jews*, XII, iii, 3.   Ezra 7 : 21, 22.

In the Hebrew text which the Septuagint translators had before them, salt is represented as always on the table of shewbread, and as an important factor in that memorial offering before the Lord. It reads: "And ye shall put upon the pile [of bread] pure frankincense and salt, and they shall be to the bread for a memorial lying before the Lord."[1] Philo Judæus makes mention of this salt with the bread, on the sacred table in the Holy Place, and refers to the salt as a symbol of perpetuity.[2]

In the directions for the preparation of the holy incense for use by the priests in the services of the tabernacle, the fragrant gums and spices were to be "seasoned [or tempered together] with salt, pure and holy."[3] And this incense was for sacrificial offering.

It is still a custom among strict Jews to observe the rite of the covenant of salt at their family table, before every meal. The head of the house, having invoked the Divine blessing in these words, "Blessed be thou O Lord our God, King of the universe, who causest bread to grow out of the earth," takes bread and breaks it in as many pieces as there are persons present. Having dipped each piece into salt, he hands a portion in turn to every one, and they share it to-

---

[1] Swete's *Septuagint* at Lev. 24 : 7.   [2] *De Victimis*, § 3.
[3] Exod. 30 : 34, 35, Revised Text, and marginal note.

gether. In cases where there is less strictness of ritual observance on the part of modern Jews, this ceremony is limited to the beginning of the Sabbath, at the Friday evening meal.

This might seem to be merely a renewal of the covenant which binds the members of the family to one another and to God; yet it evidently partakes of the nature of a sacrifice, and it is so understood by the more orthodox Jews. The primitive idea of an altar was a table of intercommunion with God, or with the gods. It was thus with the Babylonians, the Assyrians, the Egyptians, the Hindoos, the Persians, the Arabs, the early inhabitants of North and South America, and with primitive peoples generally.[1] Thus also the Bible would seem to count an altar and a table as synonymous. The prophet Malachi reproaches, in God's name, the Jews for irreverence and sacrilege. "And ye say, Wherein have we despised thy name? Ye offer polluted bread upon mine *altar*. And ye say, Wherein have we polluted thee? In that ye say, The *table* of the Lord is contemptible." [2]

The Talmud emphasizes the home table of the Jew as the altar before the Lord, to be approached in sacrifice with the essential offering of salt. "As long as

---

[1] *Blood Covenant*, pp. 167-190.
[2] Mal. 1 : 6, 7. See also Isa. 65 : 11 and Ezek. 41 : 22.

the Temple existed, the altar effected atonement, and now it is for the table of each man to effect atonement for him. It is for this reason that the description of the altar (in Ezekiel 41 : 22) closes by saying, 'And he said unto me, This is the table that is before the Lord.' " [1]

It would seem, therefore, that bread and salt are as the body and the blood, the flesh and the life, offered in sacrifice at the home table of the Jew, as formerly at the altar of intercommunion with God.[2]

This view of the household table as an altar has been recognized by many Jews. Picart [3] says:

"The German Jew sets bread and salt upon his table, but the loaf, if possible, must be whole. He cuts it without making a separation, takes it up with both his hands, sets it down upon the table, and blesses it. His guests answer, Amen. Afterwards he rubs it with salt, and whilst he is eating it is as silent as a Carthusian. The bread thus consecrated is distributed to all who are at table. If he drinks wine, he blesses it as he did the bread before ; takes it in his right hand, lifts it up, and pronounces the benediction over it; and all other drink, water alone ex-

---

[1] Tract B'rakhoth 55 a., cited by the Rev. Dr. M. Jastrow.
[2] *Blood Covenant*, pp. 350-355.
[3] *Ceremonies and Religious Customs of the Various Nations of the Known World*, I., 245. London, 1733.

cepted, is consecrated in the same manner. The master of the family concludes with Psalm 23, and then every one eats what he thinks convenient, without further ceremony. The ceremony of cutting the loaf without separation has the same reason to support it; and a passage from Psalm 10 : 3 is a voucher for its solidity. The master of the house holds the bread in both his hands, in commemoration of the ten precepts relating to corn; and each finger is the representative of one of them.[1]

"The salt as the religious intention of it is typical of the ancient sacrifices. Meat without salt has no savor, which is proved from a passage in Job, chapter 6, verse 6.[2] This is civil policy confirmed by religion.

"A modest deportment at table is much recommended; so likewise is temperance and sobriety. Their bread must be kept in a very neat place, and preserved with all imaginary care. They must talk but little, and with discretion at table, because, according to the opinion of the rabbis, the prophet Elijah, and each respective guest's guardian angel, are present at all meals. Whenever that angel hears anything indecent uttered there, he retires, and a wicked one assumes his place. They never throw down bones of flesh or fish upon the ground; but, however, this

[1] Buxtorf *ex* Talmud. [2] *Ibid.*, cap. xii.

caution is not the result of cleanliness only, but fear, lest they should hurt any of those invisible beings.[1]

"The knife that cuts their meat, must never touch what is made of milk;[2] whatever, in short, strikes the senses in any manner, must be blessed. They never rise from the table without leaving something for the poor; but the knives must be removed before they return thanks, because it is written, 'Thou shalt set no iron on the altar.' Now a table is the representative of an altar, at saying grace before, or returning thanks after meal."[3]

That the table was looked at as an altar among ancient peoples, is to be inferred from various proverbs and practices with reference to it. Thus one of the symbolic sayings of Pythagoras is, "Pick not up what is fallen from the table."[4] A comment on this is, that as the table was consecrated to divinities, whatever fell from it was not to be restored, but to be left, as was the gleaning of God's fields, for the poor.[5] When the Syrophoenician woman said to Jesus, "Yea, Lord: for even the dogs eat of the crumbs which fall from their masters' table,"[6] she

---

[1] Dr. Kohler states that the reason for not throwing these fragments on the ground, is because the Jews would not disgrace what is regarded as a special gift of God.

[2] Because meat and milk are never to be eaten together. See p. 62, *supra*. (Exod. 23:19; 34:26; Deut. 14:21.)

[3] Buxtorf *ex* Talmud, cap. xii.   [4] Dacier's *Life of Pythagoras*, p. 116.

[5] Lev. 19:9, 10; Deut. 24:19-21.   [6] Matt. 15:27.

spoke in recognition of this primitive truth, that the crumbs from the table might be shared by whoever hungered.

A usage in the early Latin Church would seem to be in the line of the Jewish thought, that bread and salt at the table are a sacrifice, or a sacrament; and it would also appear to be in recognition of the fact that salt stands for blood, or for life. The catechumens, before they were privileged to share in the Eucharist, were made partakers of the sacrament of salt (*sacramentum salis*),—salt placed in the mouth, accompanied by the sign of the cross, and by invocations and exorcisms.[1]

St. Augustine, speaking of this sacrament, says: "What they receive is holy, although it is not the body of Christ,—holier than any food which constitutes our ordinary nourishment, because it is a sacrament." And, referring to its reception by himself, he says: "I was now signed with the sign of the cross, and was seasoned with his salt."[2]

In the Greek Church, salt is still deemed an essential element of the Eucharistic bread. It is said, indeed, that the salt "represents the life, so that a

---

[1] Bingham's *Antiquities of the Christian Church*, Book X., Chap. 2; Smith and Cheetham's *Dictionary of Christian Antiequities*, arts. "Catecumens," "Salt."

[2] St. Augustine's Treatise on *Forgiveness of Sins and Baptism*, II., 46.

sacrifice without salt is but a dead sacrifice." The same is true of the Armenian and Syrian Christians. and Alcuin refers to the fact that, in his day, certain Christians in Spain insisted that salt should be put into the bread for the Eucharist.[1]

Salt is put into the mouth of an infant at its baptism, in the Roman Church of to-day.[2] In administering the salt to the babe the priest says: "Receive the salt of wisdom. May it be a propitiation for thee to eternal life."[3] All "holy water," in that church, contains salt as an essential element.[4] At the dedication of a church, water mixed with ashes and salt is employed for the sprinkling of the corners of the altar, and other portions of the church; and the remainder is poured out at the foot of the altar, where the sacrificial blood was of old poured out in the Temple offerings."[5]

In the Brâhmanas, of the Vedic literature, salt is described as the one "sacrificial essence" which is common to both sky and earth. In the ritual directions for the "ceremony of establishing a set of sacrificial fires, on the part of a young householder," the sacrificer, under the guidance of the priests, is de-

---

[1] Smith and Cheetham's *Dict. of Chris. Antiq.*, arts. "Elements," "Salt."
[2] *Rituale Romanorum*, p. 29 f. [3] *Ibid.* [4] *Ibid.*, p. 276 f.
[5] Smith and Cheetham's *Dict. of Chris. Antiq.*, art. "Salt."

SALT AS SACRIFICIAL ESSENCE 91

scribed as proceeding to equip Agni, the fire, with its proper equipments. He having brought water and gold,[1] it is said: "He then brings salt. Yonder sky assuredly bestowed that (salt as) cattle on this earth: hence they say that salt soil is suitable for cattle. That salt, therefore, means cattle; and thus he thereby supplies it (the fire) with cattle; and the latter having come from yonder (sky) is securely established on this earth. Moreover, that (salt) is believed to be the savor (*rasa*) of those two, the sky and the earth; so that he thereby supplies it (the fire) with the savor of those two, the sky and the earth. That is why he brings salt."[2]

According to the Brâhmanas, the first offered sacrifice was a man. When "the sacrificial essence" went out of the man in his offering, it went into the horse, then into the ox, then into the sheep, then into the goat. And afterwards it would seem to have been represented in salt. So in bringing salt to the fire for sacrifice, there are brought cattle, or animal offerings, with their blood and their life.[3]

It is said in Brâhmanic explanation of the pre-eminent value of salt as a sacrificial essence, that it was

---

[1] Fire is masculine, water is feminine, gold is seed, according to the Vedic literature.
[2] Müller's *Sacred Books of the East*, XII., 278 (*Satapatha Brâhmana*).
[3] *Ibid.*, p. 50.

made thus by an original agreement between the sky and the earth. "The sky and the earth were originally close together. On being separated, they said to each other, 'Let there be a common sacrificial essence (ya-*gñ*-iyam) for us!' What sacrificial essence there was belonging to yonder sky, that it bestowed on this earth, that became the salt (in the earth), and what sacrificial essence there was belonging to this earth, that it bestowed on yonder sky, that became the black (spots) in the moon. When he throws salt (on the fire-place), let him think it to be that (*viz*: the black in the moon): it is on the sacrificial essence of the sky and the earth that he sets up his fire." [1]

Among the Booddhists in China, where the sacrifices are almost exclusively vegetable, salt and wine are added in separate cups.[2] This would seem to suggest the symbolism of both blood and wine in the offerings.

Salt had its place in sacrifices in ancient Egypt. Herodotus tells, for instance, of the great annual festival at Saïs, in honor of the goddess Neith, corresponding to Athena or Minerva. Neith was, in fact, another presentation of Isis, and was known as "the great mother of all life." In conjunction with the sacrifices on this occasion, there was the Feast of

---

[1] Müller's *Sacred Books of the East*, XII., 278, note.
[2] Morris's *China and the Chinese*, p. 154.

Burning Lamps, when all the inhabitants burned, in the open air, about their houses, lamps filled with oil and salt. He says, moreover: "The Egyptians who are absent from the festival [at Saïs] observe the rite of the sacrifice, no less than the rest, by a general lighting of lamps; so that the illumination is not confined to the city of Saïs, but extends over the whole of Egypt."[1] Wilkinson says of these lamps and their contents: "The oil floated on water mixed with salt;" and he suggests a correspondence of this custom with a like one in India and in China.[2]

Friedrich, in his "Symbolism of Nature," speaking of this festival, says that the "salt symbolized the creation of life, and the light that it came forth from darkness into existence; therefore this did well suit the festival." And a collector of Etruscan remains, referring to the magic lamp still used in Italy, says, in connection with these words of Friedrich, that the "wick fire seemed so mysterious to the Rosicrucian Lord Blaize that he wrote a book on it, and on the blessed secrets of salt."[3]

Salt was essential to a sacrifice among the ancient Romans, as among the Hebrews. A cake made of coarsely ground spelt, or wheat, mingled with salt,

[1] Rawlinson's *History of Herodotus*, II., 92 (Book II., Chap. 62).
[2] *Ibid.*, note. See also Wilkinson's *Ancient Egyptians*, III., 380.
[3] Leland's *Etruscan-Roman Remains*, p. 324 f.

was broken, or bruised, and sprinkled upon the head of the victim for sacrifice, upon the fire of the altar, and upon the sacrificial knife. Hence the term "immolation," or sprinkling with this salted meal, came to be synonymous with sacrificing.[1] Pliny, telling of the priceless value of salt, says of it in conclusion: "It is in our sacred rites, more especially, that its high importance is recognized, no offering ever being made unaccompanied by the salted cake [*sine mola salso*]."[2] And Ovid says, that "in days of old it was plain spelt, and the sparkling grain of unadulterated salt that had efficacy to render the gods propitious to man."[3]

There is good reason for believing that it was much the same with the Greeks as with the Romans, although the fact that this is not distinctly declared in the classic texts has led some modern scholars to call it in question. Barley-meal cakes, with or without salt, were certainly employed by the Greeks in their sacrifices.[4] And Homer speaks of salt as "divine."[5] When, therefore, it is considered that salt was counted

[1] Harper's *Latin Dictionary*, s. vv. "Immolate," "Mola."
[2] Pliny's *Hist. Nat.*, Bostock and Riley's trans., XXXI., 41.
[3] Ovid's *Fasti*, I., 337. See, also, Cooper's *Virgil*, notes on Aeneid, Books II. and XII.
[4] Homer's *Iliad*, I., 449, 458; II., 410, 421; *Odyssey*, III., 425, 441; Philo's *Opera*, 2: 240.
[5] *Iliad*, IX., 214. See Eustathius's Commentary, I., 748-750, ed. Basle (p. 648, ed. Rome).

essential in sacrifices among the ancient Egyptians, Hindoos, and Hebrews, as also later among the Romans, it would seem to need proof to the contrary to meet the natural presumption that the Greeks also made use of "divine salt" in their sacred sacrificial cakes.

Salt was offered at every little shrine by the wayside in Guatemala, in Central America, in olden time. It was an acceptable gift to the gods.[1]

Wellhausen, in treating of the remains of Arabian paganism,[2] tells of the custom of the old priests of throwing salt into the fire of sacrifice, unperceived by the worshiper as he appealed to the gods in his oath, and of the consequent startling of the offerer by the up-leaping flames, as though under a divine impulse. Various popular sayings are cited as incidental proofs of this custom; the purport of them all being that salt in the fires of sacrifice is supposed to be an effective appeal to the gods.

Pliny says that "salt, regarded by itself, is naturally igneous, and yet it manifests an antipathy to fire, and flies from it.[3] This would seem to be a reference to the tendency of salt to spring up, or flash and sparkle, when thrown into the flames.

---

[1] See Bancroft's *Native Races of the Pacific Coast*, II., 719.
[2] Wellhausen's *Reste Arabischen Heidentumes*, in *Skizzen und Vorarbeiten*, III., 124, 131.
[3] *Hist. Nat.*, XXXI., 45.

It has indeed been suggested that the very name "salt" was derived (through *saltus*, "to leap") from the tendency of this substance "to leap and explode when thrown upon fire."[1] If there be any probability in this suggestion, or in another, and more natural one, that *saltus* was from the same root as *sal*, "salt," it is easy to see that the primitive mind might infer that such was the affinity of salt with the divine, that, when offered by fire, it leaped toward heaven, and so was understood to be peculiarly acceptable to God or to the gods, in sacrifice. The Latin verb *salis* has the twofold meaning "to salt" or "to sprinkle before sacrifice," and "to leap, spring, bound, jump;" and the root *sal* would seem to be in the Latin and the Sanskrit alike.[2] Similarly, the word "salacious," or lustful, had this origin.

It is evident that the primitive popular mind recognized salt as a peculiarly acceptable offering in sacrifice to God or the gods, and that its very name in various combinations seemed to suggest the aspiring or uprising heavenward.

[1] See citation of Lennep, and Scheideus, in Richardson's *English Dictionary*, s. v. "Salt."
[2] See Harper's *Latin Dictionary*, s. vv. "sal," "salio," "saltus."

X

SALT IN EXORCISM AND DIVINATION

X

SALT IN EXORCISM AND DIVINATION

The line between sacrificial offerings and offerings for the purpose of exorcising evil spirits, or of propitiating good spirits, is not always a clear line even in the mind of the offerer; but there are uses of salt among primitive peoples which must be placed under the head of exorcisms and divinations, and as an accompaniment of incantations, rather than under the head of sacrifices, even though they may be only perversions of the original idea of sacrifice.

Burckhardt tells of the burning of salt, by way of exorcism, among the people of Daraon, on the borders of Upper Egypt and Nubia. His caravan was about being loaded for a journey. "Just before the lading commenced," he says, "the Ababde women appeared with earthen vessels in their hands, filled with burning coals. They set them before the several loads, and threw salt upon them. At the rising of the bluish flame produced by the burning of the salt, they exclaimed, 'May you be blessed in going and in coming!' The devil and every evil genius are thus, they say, removed."[1]

Among Muhammadan Arabs, in and out of Egypt, salt is sprinkled on the floors of every apartment in the houses, on the last night of the month of Ramadan, accompanied by the words, "In the name of God, the Compassionate, the Merciful!" This is because the evil jinn, or genii, are supposed to be confined in prison during that month, and the sprinkling of salt, with the prescribed invocation, ensures protection from them as they renew their work of harm. Salt is also sprinkled on the floor after the birth of a child, as a propitiatory offering for mother and child, against the influence of the evil eye.[2]

In China, on the eve of the new year, salt is thrown into the fire, and the manner of its burning is taken as an indication, favorable or unfavorable, for the coming year. It is a species of divination by salt.[3] In Japan, the burning of salt, or the offering it in this way to the gods, is a propitiatory sacrifice in time of danger; and it is scattered at the threshold for a similar purpose after a funeral.[4] In Syria, also, the burning

---

[1] Burckhardt's *Travels in Nubia*, p. 157.
[2] Lane's *Arabian Society in the Middle Ages*, pp. 41, 188.
[3] Doolittle's *Social Life of the Chinese*, II., 58 f.
[4] Griffis's *Mikado's Empire*, pp. 467, 470; Bird's *Untrodden Tracks in Japan*, I., 392.

of a lump of salt in the fire is resorted to as a means of exorcising the malevolent spirit which afflicts one through the "evil eye."[1]

While suspected persons, or persons of doubtful orthodoxy, were undergoing the "ordeal of boiling water", under ecclesiastical authority, in the Middle Ages and earlier, it is said that "by way of extra precaution, in some ritual it is ordered that holy water and blessed salt be mingled in all the food and drink of the patient—presumably to avert diabolical interference with the result."[2]

Among the folk-lore customs in modern Greece salt has prominence in various ways. Salt must be pounded on certain days and in a certain way, in order to guard against ill luck. Salt must never be carried out of the house after dark.[3]

In Scotland and in England, as well as in the East, the use of burning salt in exorcism has continued in the more primitive regions down to the present century. James Napier tells, for example, of the treatment to which he was subjected as a child, when it was surmised that he had gotten "a blink of an ill e'e." He says: "A sixpence was borrowed from a

[1] George A. Ford, in *The Church at Home and Abroad*, Dec., 1889, p. 501.
[2] Martène, *De Antiq. Eccles. Ritibus*, Lib. III., c. vii., Ordo. 19; cited in Lea's *Superstition and Force*, p. 281.
[3] Rodd's *Customs and Lore of Modern Greece*, p. 156.

neighbor, a good fire was kept burning in the grate, the door was kept locked, and I was placed upon a chair in front of the fire. The operator, an old woman, took a tablespoon and filled it with water. With the sixpence she then lifted as much salt as it could carry, and both were put into the water in the spoon. The water was then stirred with the forefinger till the salt was dissolved. Then the soles of my feet and the palms of my hands were bathed with this solution thrice, and after these bathings I was made to taste the solution three times. The operator then drew her wet forefinger across my brow,—called 'scoring aboon the breath.' The remaining contents of the spoon she then cast over the fire, into the hinder part of the fire, saying as she did so, 'Guid preserve frae a' skith.' These were the first words permitted to be spoken during the operation."[1] Mr. Napier adds that while in his case the "scoring aboon the breath" was accomplished by scoring with a finger wet with salt water, the suspected possessor of an evil eye was scored with the finger-nails, or some sharp instrument, so as to draw blood. The blood and the salt seemed to have correspondent values.

In the southern counties of England, salt is thrown into the fire by way of invoking spiritual aid in behalf

[1] *Folk-Lore of the West of Scotland*, p. 36 f.

of a lass who would win back a recreant lover. "A pinch of salt must be thrown into the fire on three successive Friday nights, while these lines are repeated:

> "'It is not this salt I wish to burn,
> It is my lover's heart to turn;
> That he may neither rest, nor happy be,
> Until he comes and speaks to me.'"[1]

There seems to be a special value in the sacred number "three," in the appeals through salt to the spiritual powers. In the Scottish Lowlands, "when a dead body has been washed and laid out, one of the oldest women present must light a candle, and wave it three times around the corpse. Then she must measure three handfuls of common salt into an earthenware plate, and lay it on the breast. Lastly she arranges three 'toom,' or empty dishes, on the hearth, as near as possible to the fire; and all the attendants going out of the room return into it backwards, repeat this 'rhyme of saining:'

> "'Thrice the torchie, thrice the saltie,
> Thrice the dishes toom for "loffie" (*i. e.*, praise),
> These three times three ye must wave round
> The corpse, until it sleep sound.
> Sleep sound and wake nane,
> Till to heaven the soul's gane.
> If ye want that soul to dee
> Fetch the torch th' Elleree;

[1] Henderson's *Folk-Lore of the Northern Counties*, p. 176.

> Gin ye want that soul to live,
> Between the dishes place a sieve,
> An it sall have a fair, fair shrive.' "[1]

In connection with the putting of a plate of salt on the breast of a dead body, there were various usages. A plate of bread was sometimes set with the salt, and again a plate of earth was its accompaniment. And different reasons were assigned for the presence of the salt there. Napier says that many persons claimed for it a value in preventing the swelling of the body in process of decomposition, "but its original purpose was to act as a charm against the devil, to prevent him from disturbing the body." [2]

"Pennant tells us that formerly, in Scotland, the corpse being stretched on a board and covered with a close linen wrapper, the friends laid on the breast of the deceased a wooden platter, containing a small quantity of salt and earth, separate and unmixed; the earth an emblem of the corruptible body, the salt as an emblem of the immortal spirit [the life]." [3]

Napier adds: "There was an older superstition which gave another explanation for the plate of salt on the breast. There were persons calling themselves 'sin-eaters,' who, when a person died, were sent for to

---
[1] Henderson's *Folk-Lore of the Northern Counties*, p. 53.
[2] *Folk-Lore of the West of Scotland*, p. 60.
[3] Thistleton Dyer's *Domestic Folk-Lore*, p. 60.

come and eat the sins of the deceased. When they came, their *modus operandi* was to place a plate of salt and a plate of bread on the breast of the corpse, and repeat a series of incantations, after which they ate the contents of the plates, and so relieved the dead person of such sins as would have kept him hovering around his relations, haunting them with his imperfectly purified spirit, to their great annoyance, and without satisfaction to himself."[1] The basis of this plan of vicarious substitution of personality would seem to be, in the entering of the "sin-eaters" into oneness of life with the deceased through the salt covenant or the blood covenant, in partaking of his body and blood in the bread and salt from his breast.

Leland, in his "Etruscan-Roman Remains in Popular Tradition," says that there was, among the Tuscan Romans, an incantation, or an invocation, for every emergency. "If salt upset, they said, 'Dii avertite omen!'"[2] In Sicily, a goddess known as the Mother of the Day "is invoked when salt is spilt."[3] He also cites various incantations and exorcisms, in which salt is an essential factor.[4]

A custom prevails in some portions of Pennsyl-

---

[1] *Folk-Lore*, p. 60.   [2] *Etruscan-Roman Remains*, p. 12.
[3] *Ibid.*, p. 148.   [4] *Ibid.*, pp. 122, 204, 242, 264, 281, 286, 287, 312, 345.

vania, even to this day, of carrying a bag of salt, with a Bible, over the threshold, on entering a new house for the first time. There are families who would not consent to live in a home which had not been thus consecrated.[1] This would seem to be a survival of the passing over the threshold with an offering of blood. A correspondence of this practice with ancient Etruscan customs seems to be indicated by the collections of Leland.[2] Among the Mordvins, a Finnish people on the Volga, salt on bread is placed under the threshold of the bride's paternal home at the time of a marriage covenant.[3] This may be classed with sacrifices or with divination according to our idea of the workings of the primitive Mordvin mind.

[1] *Threshold Covenant*, p. 21.   [2] *Etruscan-Roman Remains*, p. 306.
[3] Ralston's *Songs of the Russian People*, p. 277 f.

XI
FAITHLESSNESS TO SALT

XI

FAITHLESSNESS TO SALT

The fact that in its primitive conception a covenant of salt is a permanent and unalterable covenant, naturally suggests to the primitive mind the idea of treachery as faithlessness to salt. The Persian term for a "traitor" is *namak harâm*, "untrue to salt," "one faithless to salt;"[1] and the same idea runs through the languages of the Oriental world.

Baron du Tott, referring to the sharing of bread and salt, says: "The Turks think it the blackest ingratitude to forget the man from whom we have received food, which is signified by the bread and salt."[2] But it is obvious that it is faithlessness to salt, not to bread or ordinary food, that is deemed blackest ingratitude. This is in India, as in Turkey. Tamerlane, the Mongol-Tatar chieftain, speaking, in his institutes, of one Share Behraum, who had deserted his service for the enemy and afterwards returned to his allegiance,

[1] Gesenius's *Thesaurus*, p. 790.
[2] *Memoirs of the Turks and Tartars*, Part I., p. 214; cited in Bush's *Illustrations of the Holy Scriptures*, at Numbers 18 : 19.

says: "At length my salt which he had eaten overwhelmed him with remorse, he again threw himself on my mercy, and humbled himself before me."[1] Frazer quotes a rebel chief in India as saying, when he capitulated after a siege, and was asked if he would return to his old allegiance, "No, I can no more visit my country; I must look for service elsewhere. I can never face the rajah again; for I have eaten Ghoorka salt. I was in trust, and I have not died at my post. We can never return to our country."[2]

Burton says that the Bed'ween of Arabia denounce the Syrians as "abusers of the salt," because they cannot be depended on in their agreements.[3] And Dr. Thomson says that Orientals "often upbraid the civilized Frank because he does not keep bread and salt, is not faithful to the covenant of brotherhood."[4]

Burton says also, of the Bed'ween of El Hejaz: "'We have eaten salt together' (*nahnu malihin*) is still a bond of friendship: there are, however, some tribes who require to renew the bond every twenty-four hours, as otherwise, to use their own phrase, 'the salt is not in their stomachs.'"[5] And he quotes the

---

[1] Quoted in Burder's *Oriental Customs*, 2d ed., p. 77.
[2] Frazer's *Journal of Tour through Himala Mountains*, quoted in Burder, p. 77, at Ezra 4 : 14.
[3] *Pilgrimage to El Medinah and Meccah*, III., 114.
[4] *The Land and the Book*, II., 41.   [5] *Pilgrimage*, III., 84.

advice to him of Shaykh Hamid, concerning the Bed'-ween who were to escort him from El Medinah, "never to allow twenty-four hours to elapse without dipping hand in the same dish with them, in order that the party might always be 'malihin,' on terms of salt."[1] Treachery on the part of one who has even partaken of an ordinary meal with another is, however, counted, among Orientals, a peculiar crime, as surprising as it is unusual.[2]

Of course, there is no human bond which will guard human nature against all possible treachery. These references to the measure of fidelity among different peoples or tribes are an indication of the relative degree of faithfulness prevailing among them severally. Those who are faithless to salt cannot be depended on for anything. If a man would not be true to one who is of his own blood, of his own life, and to whom he is bound in a sacred covenant of which his God is a party, he could not be depended on in any emergency. The covenant of salt is all this in the thought of the primitive mind.

Don Raphel says, of the estimate of faithlessness to salt entertained by Arabs generally: "When they have eaten bread and salt with any one, it would be a horrid crime not only to rob him, but even to touch

[1] *Pilgrimage*, II., 334.   [2] Psa. 41: 9; John 13: 18.

the smallest part of his baggage, or of the goods which he takes with him through the desert. The smallest injury done to his person would be considered as an equal wickedness. An Arab who should be guilty of such a crime would be looked upon as a wretch who might expect reproof and detestation from everybody. He would appear despicable to himself, and never be able to wash away his shame. It is almost unheard of for an Arab to bring such disgrace upon himself." [1]

It was said by the ancient Jews that Sodom was destroyed because its inhabitants had been faithless to salt, in maltreating guests who had partaken of salt in their city. In a Talmudic comment on Lot's wife, the record is: "Rabbi Isaac asked, 'Why did she become a pillar of salt?' 'Because she had sinned through salt. For in the night in which the men came to Lot she went to her neighbors, and said to them, Give me salt, for we have guests. But her purpose was to make (the evil-minded) people of the city acquainted with the guests. Therefore was she turned into a pillar of salt.'" [2]

This idea of foul treachery as equivalent to faithlessness in the matter of salt, seems to be perpetuated

---

[1] *The Bedouins or Arabs of the Desert*, Part II., p. 59; quoted in Burder's *Oriental Customs*, 2d ed., p. 72.

[2] Rev. Dr. Marcus Jastrow refers to this in an article on "The Symbolical Meaning of Salt," in *The Sunday School Times* for April 28, 1894.

in Da Vinci's famous painting of the Last Supper, where Judas Iscariot is represented as having overturned the salt-cellar.[1] And even among English-speaking peoples the spilling of salt between two persons is said to threaten a quarrel; as though they had already broken friendship.

Gayton, describing two friends (who were proof even against this ill sign), says :

> " I have two friends of either sex, which do
> Eat little salt, or none, yet are friends too;
> Of both which persons I can truly tell,
> They are of patience most invincible,—
> When out of temper no mischance at all
> Can put,—no, not if towards them the salt should fall."[2]

In both the Old Testament and the New faithlessness to a formal covenant is reckoned a crime of peculiar enormity as distinct from any ordinary transgression of a specific law. Transgressing a covenant with the Lord is counted on the part of Israel much the same as worshiping the gods of the heathen. This is shown in repeated instances in the Old Testa-

---

[1] It has indeed been questioned whether the overturned salt-cellar in Da Vinci's picture, as shown in many an engraving of it, was in the original painting, as it is not to be seen there now. But it would seem clear that the copy of this painting by Da Vinci's pupil, Marco d'Oggoni, in the Brera, shows the overturned salt-cellar, while the original painting has had several retouchings and renovations. (See *Notes and Queries*, 6th Series, Vol. X., p. 92 f.)

[2] Thistleton Dyer's *Domestic Folk-Lore*, p. 104.

ment.[1] In the New Testament, Paul includes among the grossest evil-doers of paganism those who are "filled with all unrighteousness, wickedness, covetousness, maliciousness; full of envy, murder, strife, deceit, malignity; whisperers, backbiters, hateful to God," and so down to "covenant-breakers," and those "without natural affection," as among the lowest and worst of all.[2] This idea shows itself continually in records and traditions, sacred and secular.

[1] Gen. 17 : 14; Deut. 17 : 2-7; Josh. 7 : 11-15; Judg. 2 : 20-23; 2 Kings 18 : 11, 12; Psa. 55 : 19-21; Isa. 24 : 5, 6; Jer. 11 : 9-11; 34 : 17-20; Hosea 6 : 4-7; 8 : 1.
[2] Rom. 1 : 31.

XII
SUBSTITUTE TOGETHER WITH REALITY

XII

SUBSTITUTE TOGETHER WITH REALITY

Primarily it is the blood, as the life, of two persons entering into a covenant with each other and with the Author of life, that is the nexus of the enduring covenant.[1] Secondarily, it is the blood, or life, of a substitute victim offered as a sacrifice to God, or to the gods, that is accepted as such a nexus,—the blood being shared by the contracting parties, or being poured out as an oblation to God, and the flesh being eaten conjointly by the parties covenanting.[2]

Yet, again, wine is accepted as representing blood. This is not only because wine resembles blood in appearance, and is called in the Bible record the "blood of the grape,"[3] but because wine is actually deemed, by many primitive peoples, real blood, and is supposed to affect its users as it does because it represents the spirit, or life, of the divinity whose blood it is.[4] On this point Frazer calls attention to

[1] *Blood Covenant*, pp. 5-86; *Threshold Covenant*, pp. 193-202.
[2] Gen. 4 : 2-5; *Blood Covenant*, pp. 134-136.
[3] Gen. 49 : 11; Deut. 32 : 14; Eccles. 39 : 26; 50 : 15; 1 Macc. 6 : 34; *Blood Covenant*, p. 191. [4] *Blood Covenant*, pp. 139-142.

the primitive views of Egyptians, Arabians, Aztecs, and others, citing authorities from Plutarch to Robertson Smith.[1]

He says, for example : "We are informed by Plutarch that of old the Egyptian kings neither drank wine nor offered it in libations to the gods, because they held it to be the blood of beings who had once fought against the gods, the vine having sprung from their rotting bodies ; and the frenzy of intoxication was explained by the supposition that the drunken man was filled with the blood of the enemies of the gods. The Aztecs regarded *pulque*, or the wine of the country, as bad, on the account of the wild deeds which men did under its influence. But these wild deeds were believed to be the acts, not of the drunken man, but of the wine god by whom he was possessed and inspired. . . . Thus it appears that, on the primitive view, intoxication, or the inspiration produced by wine, is exactly parallel to the inspiration produced by drinking the blood of animals.[2] The soul or life is in the blood, and wine is the blood of the vine. . . . Whoever drinks wine drinks the blood, and so receives into himself the soul or spirit of the god of the vine."

Naturally, a substitute or representative of the

---

[1] Frazer's *Golden Bough*, II., 184 f.
[2] Comp. *Blood Covenant*, pp. 114, 139-147.

original, or real, nexus of a covenant, came to stand for the primary article with such prominence in the popular mind that it would be deemed an essential, not only when the real was lacking, but while the real was actually present. Therefore we find libations of wine accompanying actual blood, in sacrifices,[1] as well as used in substitution for it; so also of other substitutes, such as saffron water, milk, and coffee, at other times.[2]

As salt represents blood and life, quite naturally salt is employed in sacrifices, not only where there is no blood or life, but also where there is. And this accounts for the prominence of salt in sacrifices, and elsewhere, where blood or life is essential as a fitting offering, and as a bond of union.[3] Both wine and salt as substitutes for blood are frequently used together, as though one alone were not sufficient.[4]

Similarly, bread is a recognized representative of flesh. It is so understood in sacred and secular records and traditions. When Jesus spoke of bread as his flesh, and as his body,[5] and of the fruit of the vine as his

---

[1] Exod. 29: 40; Lev. 23: 12, 13; Num. 15: 5, 10; 28: 14, etc.; *Blood Covenant*, pp. 63-65.   [2] *Blood Covenant*, pp. 77, 346-350.

[3] Herodotus, Plutarch, and Pliny, cited in Becker's *Charicles*, p. 330.

[4] See pp. 83 f., 92, *supra;* also Frazer's *Golden Bough*, II., 67-70.

[5] Comp. Matt. 26: 26-28; Mark 14: 22-24; Luke 22: 19, 20; 1 Cor. 11: 23-25.

blood, he used terms that in his day, and earlier, were known in popular thought as representing the truth at the basis of the covenant by which two became one in a merged common life.[1] Yet while bread was an accepted substitute for flesh, it was much used as an accompaniment of flesh[2] in sacrificial feasts. Thus bread and salt as recognized substitutes for flesh and blood came to be commonly used even where real flesh and blood were the main factors in the sacrifice. Substitutes for bread, such as honey and flour or meal, were, as already shown, also used in connection with bread. Hence it is not unnatural to find salt as blood accompanying blood itself. This is entirely in accord with primitive thought and customs generally.

[1] *Blood Covenant*, pp. 171-184.
[2] *Ibid.;* Gen. 18 : 1-8; 31 : 54; Lev. 7 : 11-14; 23 : 15-20, etc.

XIII
ADDED TRACES OF THE RITE

XIII

ADDED TRACES OF THE RITE

On the occasion of a sacred alliance between clans, or in a treaty of peace at the close of a war, among the Kookies of India, there is a formal appeal to the gods, in which salt has an important part. A *dhar*, or short sword, is placed on the ground between the two parties. On it, as on an altar, "are arranged rice, salt, earth, fire, and a tiger's tooth. The party swearing takes the *dhar* and puts the blade between his teeth, and, biting it, says, 'May I be cut with the *dhar* in war and in the field; may rice and salt fail me, my crops wither, and I die of hunger; may fire burn all my worldly possessions, and the tiger devour me, if I am not faithful!'"[1]

Among the Battas, in Sumatra, the more solemn form of their oath is, "May my harvest fail, my cattle die, and may I never taste salt again, if I do not speak the truth."[2]

[1] Stewart, in *Journal of the Asiatic Society of Bengal*, XXIV., 641, cited in Spencer's *Descriptive Sociology*, V., 39.

[2] Wooldridge's trans. of Bunge's *Physiological and Pathological Chemistry*, p. 126.

Among the Dyaks of Borneo, when a question arises between disputants for which there is no ordinary mode of settlement, each litigant is given a lump of salt, which the two drop into water simultaneously, and he whose lump dissolves soonest is adjudged the loser.[1]

In the Kenyah tribe in Borneo, the ceremony of naming a child is made much of. Guests assemble on the occasion. After the more private ceremony, participated in by a favored few, every guest present is given a package of salt and some ginger root, as wedding-cake is given in many lands, for a souvenir of the occasion.[2]

A custom among Slavic peoples of presenting bread and salt to a ruler at the threshold of his domain, as he comes on a visit, would seem to combine the two ideas of hospitality and of worship. When the Emperor of Russia visits one of his provinces, or subject cities, he is met at its threshold by its representative rulers, as his loyal subjects, with bread and salt served on a golden or a silver-gilt placque. In the Winter Palace of St. Petersburg there are hundreds of these suspended over the doorways and on the walls, which

---

[1] Köningswarter, *op. cit.*, p. 202, cited in Henry C. Lea's *Superstition and Force*, p. 257.

[2] On the testimony of Dr. W. H. Furness, 3d.

placques were thus presented to different emperors on the occasion of such visits.

When the Grand Duke Alexis visited America in 1872, he was received in this way by the wife of the Russian Minister at Washington. "As the Grand Duke entered the Legation, Madame de Catacazy carried a silver salver on which was placed a round loaf of plain black bread, on the top of which was imbedded a golden salt-cellar."[1] This was obviously more than a symbol of welcome to the home of the embassy. The Grand Duke came as a ruler and lord to his own, and his own received him loyally, with symbols of reverent submission. It was more like the threshold covenant of the East, when blood is poured out from an offered body at the doorway of a house, as one who would be honored as well as welcomed comes in.

Some years later there was an account in the London Court Journal of the making in Paris of an ornate golden dish for a similar use in Roumania. The burghers of Bucharest were arranging to present on this dish bread and salt to Princess Marie of Edinburgh, when she should make her first entrance into their city as their future queen. The dish was of gold

[1] Perley's *Reminiscences of Sixty Years in the National Metropolis*, II., 277.

worked in a purely Renaissance design, its edge being an openwork pattern of interlaced ears of corn and branches of laurel. In the center was the salt-cellar, shaped like an open tulip, and resting upon four graceful stalks.

In the days of Queen Elizabeth of England it was a custom of officials of the palace to rub bread and salt on the plates of the dining-table before each royal meal.[1]

Among the Kookies of the Hill Tribes in India, "whenever they send any message of consequence to each other, they always put in the hand of the bearer of it a small quantity of salt, to be delivered with the message as expressive of its importance."[2] This would seem to indicate a life-and-death matter in the message.

An old English custom of having a salt-cellar at a certain point on the family table, and of seating those present above or below it, gave rise to the phrase "sitting below the salt" as indicative of an inferior position at the household table. As salt was a symbol of hospitality and of covenanted union, he who was within the scope of salt-sharing at a table was in

---

[1] Agnes Strickland, *Queens of England* (Students' Edition), p. 403.

[2] Macrae, in *Asiatic Researches*, VII., 188; cited in Spencer's *Descriptive Sociology*, V. 25.

a very different position from one who was outside of it.

A reference to this custom by Sir Walter Scott, in his "Tales of My Landlord," in the first quarter of the nineteenth century, provoked much discussion, and doubt was expressed as to the existence of the custom in olden time. But abundant evidence was produced as to its veritableness.[1] An old English ballad was cited, in which one said sneeringly to his inferior:

> "Thou art a carle mean of degree,
> Ye salte doth stand twain me and thee;
> But an thou hadst been of ane gentyl strayne,
> I wold have bitten my gant[2] aganie."

And one of Bishop Hall's Satires, in 1597, was instanced as saying:

> "A gentle squire would gladly entertaine
> Into his house some trencher chaplaine;
> Some willing man that might instruct his sons,
> And that would stande to good conditions.
> First, that he lie upon the truckle-bed,
> Whiles his young maister lieth o'er his head.
> Second, that he do, on no default,
> Ever presume to sit above the salt."

It was a custom in Oxford University to give salt to a student who had concluded his course as a "freshman," and was finding admission into the company

---

[1] See *Blackwood's Magazine*, Vol. I., No. 1, pp. 33-35; 132-134; 349-352; 579-582.
[2] Gant; that is, glove.

of maturer, or salter, students or sophisters. Drinking salt and water, or salt and beer, was a part of this ceremony. It was called "salting a freshman," or "college salting."[1]

A series of plates, illustrative of certain student ceremonies at Strassburg University was published in 1666. "The last [of these] represents *the giving of the salt*,—which a person is holding on a plate in his left hand, and with his right hand is about to put a pinch of it upon the tongue of each *becanus*, or freshman. A glass, probably holding wine, is standing near him. Underneath is the following couplet:

"*Sal Sophiæ gustate, bibatis vinaque læta,
Augeat immensus vos in utrisque Deus!*"[2]

In Hungary, at a wedding, there are customs that give solemn emphasis to the truth that two lives are newly made one in a sacred covenant. The ceremony is presided over by the Vajda, or chief ruler, rather than by any Christian ecclesiastic. He stands with his back to a blazing fire as the primitive altar.[3] When his address is concluded, an earthen vessel is dashed to pieces as a symbol of their former life now ended. Then the bridal couple are sprinkled with

---

[1] See *Notes and Queries*, First Series, I., 261. [2] *Ibid.*, I., 492.
[3] *Threshold Covenant*, pp. 22 f., 39 ff., etc.

salt and brandy, doubly standing for blood on the threshold of their married life.[1]

Bread and salt seem to have a peculiar sacredness among the Hungarian gypsies. This incident, from a gypsy camp, is given in a Hungarian newspaper: A gypsy who had lost his cash informed his leader of the fact, and at once an order was issued for its restoration. The money not appearing, the gypsy chief bound two poles into the form of a cross, and fixed one end in the ground. On the top of the cross he fastened a piece of bread, and sprinkled it with salt. Each member of the band was then called to swear upon this symbol that he had not committed the theft. All stood the test, until the last one, an old woman, came forward. As she was about to take the oath, she turned pale, put her hand in her pocket, and brought out the stolen money. She was then soundly beaten, and kicked out of camp.[2]

The primitive idea that the sovereign properly controls salt as a source or means of life, and that a gift of salt from the sovereign lays a new obligation on the recipient, as illustrated in the days of Cyrus and Darius,[3] shows itself down to our own day. In the

---

[1] *Martyrdom of an Empress*, p. 138 f.
[2] See quotation from the Pester Lloyd, in *Journal of the Gypsy Folklore Society*, copied in "The Journal of American Folk-lore," Vol. II., No. 5, p. 140.   [3] See p. 20, *supra*.

days of Arabi Pasha, the Khedive of Egypt desired to raise a sum of money, at a time when the people were exceptionally poor in consequence of excessive taxation and the rigors of a recent famine. Instead of relying on the ordinary and obnoxious tax collectors, the Khedive resorted to the pressure of the "fidelity to salt idea."

Salt, as a gift, or as an appeal, from the government supply, was sent to every native house. Four pecks of salt to every two males in the house was the average amount. The salt was laid, by a government official, upon the threshold of the house, early in the morning, before the inmates arose. Of course, any person stepping over that salted threshold was brought anew into a covenant with the giver.[1] Later in the day Egyptian soldiers called at every house to receive what the inmates would give in return. The appeal was irresistible. It was not like an ordinary tax, to be evaded or resisted if possible. All would do what they could. The least that any could think of returning was the usual price of the salt. Those who could afford more were glad to show their fidelity and loyalty in a corresponding liberality.[2]

---

[1] See *Threshold Covenant*, pp. 3-25.

[2] This was told to the author by an Oriental who was residing in Egypt at the time.

XIV
A SAVOR OF LIFE OR OF DEATH

XIV

A SAVOR OF LIFE OR OF DEATH

That which is a means of life in one instance may be a means of death in another. A breath that might kindle a tiny spark into a living blaze might also extinguish a quivering flame. The breeze that gives life to fire in one case gives death to fire in the other. And fire itself proves death to that which is perishable, while it gives added value to that which is purified in the furnace flames. Salt, like fire, is a symbol both of life and of death. In different connections it is a preserver and a destroyer. "To the one a savor from death unto death; to the other a savor from life unto life."[1]

Salt is spoken of in the Bible as destructive of vegetable life, and a barrier against new animal life. A piece of ground sown or strewed with salt is deemed dead land: "It is not sown, nor beareth, nor any grass groweth therein."[2] When Abimelech captured Shechem, "he beat down the city and sowed

[1] 2 Cor. 2 : 16.   [2] Deut. 29 : 23.

it with salt."[1] The Psalmist, speaking of the power and ways of God, declares :

> "He turneth rivers into a wilderness,
> And watersprings into a thirsty ground ;
> A fruitful land into a salt desert,
> For the wickedness of them that dwell therein."[2]

The prophet Jeremiah says of one who departs from God's service that he "shall inhabit the parched places in the wilderness, a salt land and not inhabited."[3] Ezekiel, foretelling a curse on the land of the Jews, says : "The marshes thereof shall not be healed ; they shall be given up to salt."[4] And Zephaniah declares that Moab shall become "a possession of nettles, and salt-pits, and a perpetual desolation."[5] Because there can be no fertility for new vegetable life, there is no room or hope for new animal life for land thus sown with salt and thus permanently sterile.

The one great body of water that is called the Dead Sea is the saltest sea in the world. Five times the proportion of salt in the ocean is found in this inland sea of salt. "No fish can exist in the waters, nor is it proved that any low forms of life have been discovered there."[6] An ancient legend declared that birds could not even fly over its waters, because of

---

[1] Judg. 9 : 45.   [2] Psa. 107 : 33, 34.   [3] Jer. 17 : 6.
[4] Ezek. 47 : 11.   [5] Zeph. 2 : 9.
[6] George Adam Smith's *Historical Geography of the Holy Land*, p. 502.

the curse from heaven on its briny depths.¹ Yet this doomed and dead sea of salt is a source of life to man in its exhaustless supply of salt for his use. Preeminently is this salt of the Dead Sea a savor of life and of death.

The salt of the ocean is the world's treasure. Without it the greater portion of the earth's inhabitants would perish for lack of what vivifies and preserves animal life. Yet because of the salt in the ocean the very water, which man and beast must have or perish of thirst, is useless to both man and beast. The cry in the "Ancient Mariner" is the cry of the human, always, on the ocean's surface:

> "Water, water, everywhere,
> And all the boards did shrink:
> Water, water, everywhere,
> Nor any drop to drink."

Water, which is the gift of God to the thirsty soul, mocks the thirsty soul when it brings with it salt, which is the representative of life. Salt in water is a savor of death unto death, while salt and water are also a savor of life unto life.

While salt as the equivalent of life is a symbol of permanency, it becomes, as the equivalent of death, a symbol of doom and destruction. Thus the prophet

---

[1] Tacitus, *Hist.*, v. 6, cited as above.

Isaiah, speaking of his salvation as sure and permanent, says: "Lift up your eyes to the heavens, and look upon the earth beneath: for the heavens shall vanish away [literally, shall be salted] like smoke, and the earth shall wax old like a garment, and they that dwell therein shall die in like manner [or, like gnats]: but my salvation shall be forever, and my righteousness shall not be abolished." [1]

Life is in itself the destroyer of death, as light is the destroyer of darkness. Hence that which makes anew does away with that which was of old. When, therefore, salt or fire is spoken of as the destroyer of that which is not worthy of preservation, it is not to be wondered at that this power is possessed by an element that purifies and revivifies through the process of destruction. The ground of a destroyed and condemned city is guarded against a continuance of its old life of evil by being sown with salt, which is a savor from life unto life and from death unto death. The old heavens and the old earth which vanish away as by fire and salt,[2] are replaced by a new heaven and a new earth [3] which shall be enduring as gold tried in the fire, and as a covenant of salt forever.

There is a sense in which that which is devoted to

---

[1] Isa. 51:6.   [2] Isa. 34:4; 2 Peter 3:10-12.
[3] Isa. 51:16; 65:17; 66:22; 2 Peter 3:13.

God is thereby forbidden to the use of man. Thus land sown with salt may be counted as devoted and as destroyed, *devoted* to God and *destroyed* for man.[1] The Hebrew word *korban* was applied to what had thus been dedicated and doomed.[2]

Blood also is used in the twofold sense of life and of death, in different connections. Men say, "We are bound together by blood," and "We are of one blood," and "Blood is thicker than water." They say, also, "There is blood between us," and "Spilled blood cannot be gathered up," and "Blood is a barrier." Salt, that stands for blood, may similarly stand for life or for death, for peace or for discord. It is an old superstition that to put salt on another's plate is an evil omen. Hence the couplet:

"Help me to salt,
Help me to sorrow!"

Yet even this portent of ill luck may be canceled by a repetition of the act, helping to a second portion of salt.[3] The taking of blood that becomes a barrier may be followed by the taking of blood as a bond of union. Shedding of blood is atoned for by sharing of blood.

[1] See Num. 21 : 2, 3.
[2] Mark 7 : 11. See the Rev. Dr. Jastrow, in *The Sunday School Times* for April 28, 1894; also W. Robertson Smith's *Religion of the Semites*, p. 435; also Nowack, *Lehrbuch der Hebraeischen Archäologie*, II., 267.
[3] Henderson's *Folk-Lore of the Northern Counties*, p. 120. Thistleton Dyer's *Domestic Folk-Lore*, p. 104 f.

Even the spilling of salt, which is so dreaded in primitive thought, may, it is said, be rendered harmless if the person who was guilty of the mishap will carefully gather up the spilled salt with the blade of a knife, and throw it over his left shoulder, with an appropriate invocation.[1]

It is deemed dangerous to give away salt to a stranger; for because salt is as blood and as life, one must be careful lest he put his blood and his life in the power of an enemy.[2] Salt is essential to the preservation of human life; at the same time, salt is the destruction of human life if it be in too great quantity or proportion. Thus the seeming contradiction is only in seeming.

[1] Henderson, p. 120; Dyer, p. 104 f.; Napier, p. 139 f.
[2] Henderson, p. 217.

XV
MEANS OF A MERGED LIFE

XV

MEANS OF A MERGED LIFE

All life is from the Author and Source of life. Only as two persons become partakers of a common life by each and both sharing in that which is in itself life, can they become one in the all-inclusive Life. Having life from the Source of life, they can merge their common possession in each other, and in that common Source. Such merging in a common life, with an appeal to and by the approval of God, or the gods, has been the root-idea of covenanting, in one way or another, from time immemorial, among all peoples, the world over.

In primitive thought, and in a sense in scientific fact, the blood is the life and the life is in the blood; hence they who share in each other's blood are sharers in a merged and common life. Covenanting in this way with a solemn appeal to God, or to the gods, has been a mode of sacred union from the earliest dawn of human history. Two thus covenanting are supposed to become of one being; the one is the other, and the two are one. Every form of sacrifice, Jewish, Egyptian, Assyrian, or ethnic, is in its primal thought either an evidence and a reminder of an existing covenant between the offerer and the Deity approached, or an appeal and an outreaching for a covenant to be consummated.[1]

Salt is counted as the equivalent of blood and of life, both in primitive thought and, in a sense, in scientific fact; therefore salt, like blood, has been deemed a nexus of a lasting covenant, as nothing can be which is not life or its equivalent. Only as two persons are sharers of a common life can they be supposed to have merged their separate identity in that dual union.

And so we find that, in the primitive world's thought, shared salt has preciousness and power because of what it represents and of what it symbolizes, as well as of what it is. Salt stands for and corresponds with, and it symbolizes, blood and life. As such it represents the supreme gift from the Supreme Giver. Because of this significance of salt, when made use of as the means of a lasting union, the Covenant of Salt, as a form or phase of the Blood Covenant, is a covenant fixed, permanent, and unchangeable, enduring forever.

[1] Compare, for example, Psa. 50 : 5, 16; Hos. 1 : 10; Rom. 9 : 26.

SUPPLEMENT

THE TEN COMMANDMENTS AS A COVENANT OF LOVE

THE TEN COMMANDMENTS AS A COVENANT OF LOVE

All of us are familiar with the Ten Commandments, given from God on two tables, or tablets, of stone, to the people of Israel at Mount Sinai.[1] But not all of us are accustomed to think of these Ten Commandments as ten separate clauses of a loving covenant between God and his chosen people, recorded on stone tablets for their permanent preservation. Yet these witnessing tablets are repeatedly called in the Bible "the tables of the covenant,"[2] and "tables of testimony,"[3] not the tables of the commandments; while the chest or casket which contained them is called "the ark of the covenant,"[4] and "the ark of the testimony,"[5] not the ark of the commandments.

There is obviously a world-wide difference between

[1] Exod. 20 : 1-17; Deut. 5 : 1-22. [2] Deut. 9 : 15.
[3] Exod. 32 : 15; 34 : 29.
[4] Num. 14 : 44; Deut. 10 : 8; 31 : 9, 25, 26; Josh. 3 : 3, 6, 8, 11, 14, 17; 4 : 7, 9, 18; 6 : 6, 8; 8 : 33; Judg. 20 : 27; 1 Sam. 4 : 3-5; 2 Sam. 15 : 24; 1 Kings 3 : 15; 6 : 19; 8 : 1, 6; 1 Chron. 15 : 25, 26, 28, 29; 16 : 6, 37; 17 : 1; 22 : 19; 28 : 2, 18; 2 Chron. 5 : 2, 7; Jer. 3 : 16.
[5] Exod. 25 : 22; 26 : 33, 34; 30 : 6, 26; 31 : 7; 39 : 35; 40 : 3, 5, 21; Num. 4 : 5; 7 : 89; Josh. 4 : 16.

a loving covenant that binds two parties to each other in mutual affection and fidelity, and a series of arbitrary commandments enjoined by a sovereign upon his subjects; between a compact of union, having its statement of promises on the one hand and of responsibilities on the other, and an instrument that asserts the rights of the ruler and defines the duties of the ruled. In our estimate of the Decalogue we have made too much of the *law* element, and too little of the element of *love*. As a consequence it has not been easy for us to see how it is that God's law is love, and that love is the fulfilling of God's law. But the Ten Commandments *are* a simple record of God's loving covenant with his people, and they are *not* the arbitrary commandings of God to his subjects. They indicate the inevitable limits within which God and his people can be in loving union, rather than declare the limits of dutiful obedience on the part of those who would be God's faithful subjects. A close examination of the Decalogue will show that this is its nature and scope.

It must be borne in mind, in our Bible reading, that the Bible was originally written by Orientals for Orientals, and that it is to be looked at in the light of Oriental manners and customs, and Oriental modes of speech, in order to its fullest understanding. Hence when we find the term "covenant," or the term "commandment," in the Bible, we are to inquire into the Oriental meaning of that term, so that we may know the sense in which it was employed by the Bible writers.

Now a "covenant" among Orientals is, and always has been, a sacred compact binding two parties in loving agreement. Oriental covenants are made in various forms and by various ceremonies. The most sacred of all forms of covenanting in the East is by two persons commingling their own blood, by its drinking or by its inter-transfusing, in order that they may come into a communion of very life.[1] Two persons who wish to become as one in a loving blood-friendship will open each a vein in his own arm, and allow the blood to flow into a common vessel, from which both parties will drink of the commingled blood. Or, again, each person will open a vein in one of his hands, and the bleeding hands will be clasped together so that the blood from the one shall find its way into the veins of the other. Or, yet again, the two will share together the substitute blood of a sacred animal. Usually, in such a case, a written compact is signed by each party and given to the other, with the stamp of the writer's blood upon it as

[1] See *The Blood Covenant.*

a part of the ceremony of covenanting; and this writing is carefully encased in a small packet or casket, and guarded by its holder as his very life. It is in the light of such customs as this that we are to read of the sacred covenant entered into between God and his Oriental people.

It was at the foot of Mount Sinai that Moses came before the people of Israel with God's proffer to them of a covenant, whereby they should bear his name and be known as his people. "And he took the book of the covenant, and read in the audience of the people: and they said, All that the Lord hath spoken will we do, and be obedient."[1] Then it was that Moses took of substitute blood and divided it into two portions, one half to be sprinkled on the altar Godward, and the other half to be sprinkled on the people; and Moses said: "Behold the blood of the covenant, which the Lord hath made with you concerning all these words"—or, as the margin of the Revised Version has it, "upon all these conditions."[2]

Moreover, we are told, in the Epistle to the Hebrews,[3] that Moses sprinkled the blood upon the record, or book, of the covenant, as well as upon the people. It was after this—after the breach and the renewal of the covenant between Israel and God—

---

[1] Exod. 24 : 7.   [2] Exod. 24 : 8.   [3] Heb. 9 : 19.

that the stone tablets on which the covenant itself had a permanent record were encased in a casket, or an "ark,"[1] which was thenceforward guarded sacredly as containing the charter of Israel's nationality, the witness, the evidence, the testimony, of the loving covenant between God and his people.

But you may ask, Did not the tables of stone bear a record of specific commandments, rather than of articles of a covenant? And are not the words there recorded specifically called in the Bible the "Ten Commandments"? Look for yourselves, and see. It is true that our English Bible speaks of the Ten Commandments recorded on these tables of stone; but the word here translated "commandments" is more literally to be rendered "words,"[2] as indeed it is given in the margin of the Revised Version; and it is applicable to any declaration, injunction, or charge, made by one to another. It is by no means to be understood as simply an arbitrary mandate from an absolute sovereign to his subjects. Looking at the Ten Commandments as a set of moral laws covering man's duties to God and to his fellows, they seem strangely defective, when we find among them no command to pray to or to praise God, nor any command to give sympathy or assistance to man. But

[1] Exod. 40 : 20. [2] Exod. 34 : 28.

when we look at them as clauses of a loving covenant, indicating the scope and limits of relations within which a child of God's duties God-ward and man-ward are to be exercised, we find that they are far-reaching and all-inclusive. Looking at them as the tables of the covenant between God and his people in the light of Oriental views of covenanting, we can see a great deal more in the words on those tables than when we look at them as the tables of the commandments,—in the light of our Western ideas of commandings.

A covenant involves the idea of a twofold agreement between the parties making it. Even though God himself be one of the parties, he will not refuse to be explicit in his words of covenanting. And so we find it to be in the record on the tables of the covenant which were given to Moses at Mount Sinai. We call the opening words of that record the "Preface to the Ten Commandments;" but they are more properly God's covenanting words with his people. "I am Jehovah thy God, which brought thee out of the land of Egypt, out of the house of bondage."[1] The very name "Jehovah" includes the idea of a covenant-making and a covenant-keeping God. The declaration of Jehovah's eternally existing personality

[1] Exod. 20 : 2.

as Jehovah is in itself a covenant promise, for all time to come, to those who are his covenant people. It is as though he were to say : "I, who was and am, and am to be, the same yesterday and to-day, yea and forever, will be your God unfailingly. As I have given you a loving deliverance out of Egyptian bondage, so I am ever ready to deliver you from every evil that enthralls you."

Man, when he promises for the future, needs to say, "I will do ;" but God can say nothing stronger than "I do," or than "I am." Thus the promise of promises of Jesus to his disciples as their ever-present, all-sustaining Lord, is, "Lo, I am with you alway ;"[1] not "Lo, I *will be*," but "Lo, I *am*." And so it is that God's covenant promise to Israel, to be their loving, guarding, and guiding God for all time to come, is in the words : "I am Jehovah thy God, which brought thee out of the land of Egypt, out of the house of bondage."[2] And this is the promise of "the party of the first part," as we would say in modern legal parlance, in this covenant between God and his people Israel.

Then there follow the covenant agreements of God's people, as "the party of the second part" in this loving compact. As it is God who prescribes or

[1] Matt. 28 : 20. [2] Exod. 20 : 2.

defines the terms on which this covenant is to be made, the indication of those terms is mainly in the form of such prohibitions as will distinguish the people of God from other peoples about them, in the bearing of that people toward God's personality, toward God's institutions, and toward God's representatives. This is all that is needed in the fundamental articles of covenanting. The details of specific duties may be defined in special enactments under the terms of this covenant, or they may be inferred from its spirit.

The first requirement is, that this covenanting God shall be recognized as the only God ; that no other god shall be conceded a place in God's universe. And this requirement is vital to any such covenant. A divided heart is no heart at all. He who can see any other object of love and devotion comparable with the one to whom he gives himself in covenant-union, is thereby incapacitated from a covenant-union. Therefore it is that this first word of the Ten Words of the covenant of God's people with their God is not an arbitrary mandate, but is the simple expression of a truth which is essential to the very existence of the covenant as a covenant of union.

And this principle is as vitally important now as it was in the days of Moses. The human heart is always inclined to divide itself when it ought to be undivided. It is reluctant to be wholly and always true to God alone. But, now as hitherto, without wholeness of heart a covenant of union with God is an impossibility. And, indeed, the very idea of other gods is an outgrowth of man's sense of an unfitness to be in oneness of life with the One God,—in consequence of which man seeks a lower divinity than the supreme God as the immediate object of his worship.

The second requirement in this covenant of union is, that no material image or representation of this covenanting God shall be made use of as a help to his worship by his covenanting people ; that, as a Spirit, God shall be worshiped in spirit by his people. Here, again, is no arbitrary mandate, but only the recognition of a vital truth. Because God is Creator of all, no creation of God can be like God. Because God is a Spirit, the human mind can best commune with him spiritually, without having its conceptions of him degraded by any image or representation—which at the best must be wholly unworthy of him.

In this second requirement, as in the first, a danger is indicated to which the Israelites were peculiarly exposed in their day, and to which all the people of God are exposed in any day. In the Assyrian, or Chaldean, home of Abraham, there was practically no image worship, but there was a belief in a plurality of gods. In the Egyptian home, from which the Israelites had just come out, images in great variety were the objects of worship. As the covenant people of God, the Israelites were to refrain from the polytheism of their ancestral home in the far East, and from the grosser idolatry of their more recent home in the West. And so it must be with the people of God at all times; they must worship only God, and they must worship God without any help from a material representation of the object of their worship.

As there is still a temptation to give a divided heart to God, so there is still a temptation to seek the help of some visible representation or symbol of God's presence in his worship. The Christian believer does not bow down to an idol, but many a Christian believer thinks that his mind can be helped upward in worship by looking at some representation of his Saviour's face, or at some symbol of his Saviour's passion. But just because God is infinitely above all material representations and symbols, so God can best be apprehended and discerned spiritually. Anything coming between man's spirit and God the Spirit is a hindrance to worship, and not a help to it. Suppose a young man were watching from a window for his absent mother's return, with a wish to catch the first glimpse of her approaching face. Would he be wise, or foolish, in putting up a photograph of his mother on the window-pane before him, as a help to bearing her in mind as he looks for her coming? As there can be no doubt about the answer to that question, so there can be no doubt that we can best come into spiritual communion with God by closing our eyes to everything that can be seen with the natural eye, and opening the eyes of our spirit to the sight of God the Spirit. This, again, is no arbitrary requirement of God; it is in the very nature of his being and of our own.

The third requirement of this compact is, that there shall be no insincerity on the part of God's covenant people in their claiming and bearing his name, as the name of their covenanting God. This requirement is not generally understood in this light; but all the facts in the case go to show that this is its true light. In the Oriental world, and in the primitive world everywhere, one's name stands for one's personality; and the right to bear one's name or even to call on one by his personal name, is a proof of intimate relation, if not of actual union, with him. God was now covenanting with this people to be his people, thereby authorizing them to bear his name, and to be known as his representatives. In the very nature of things, this laid upon them a peculiar obligation to bear his name reverently and in all sincerity.

It is not that God arbitrarily commanded his people to have a care in the *speaking* of his name, as if he were jealous of its irreverent mention ; but it is that he reminded them that the coming into the privileges of his name was the coming into the responsibilities of that name. It was as though Mr. Moody were taking a little street waif into his home to train the boy as his own son, and were formally giving to that boy the right to take and bear his name. Naturally he might say : "Understand, now, my boy, that, wherever you go, they'll say, 'There goes a young Moody.' Now, I value my name, and I don't want it disgraced. See to it that you take care of that name wherever you are." So God said to his people : "Thou shalt not take"—shalt not assume, bear, carry—"the name of the Lord thy God in vain"—insincerely, vainly ; "for the Lord will not"—cannot— "hold him guiltless that taketh"—claimeth the privileges of—"his name in vain"—vainly, insincerely.

This covenant obligation also is on us as it was on God's people of old. As Christians we are baptized into the name of the Father, the Son, and the Holy Ghost.[1] Wherever we go, we are counted as mem-

[1] Matt. 28 : 19.

bers of God's family. His name is on us, and his honor is in our keeping. Wherefore, "let every one that nameth the name of the Lord"—claimeth it as his own name—"depart from unrighteousness;"[1] and let him never feel that it is a light or a vain thing to bear that name before the world.

Thus we see that the first three of the ten requirements of the loving covenant of God's people with their God are simply the requirements to worship God as the only God, to worship him in unhindered spirituality, and to worship him in all sincerity. These three fundamental requirements seem to have been in the mind of our Lord Jesus when he said to the woman of Samaria at the well of Jacob: "God"—the One God—"is a Spirit: and they that worship him must worship in spirit and truth."[2]

Coming to the fourth requirement of the loving covenant of God and his people, we find it differing in form from the preceding three requirements; differing also from the form of all but one of those which follow it. The preceding three are in the negative form; this is in the affirmative form, beginning with the injunction, "Remember" (Keep in mind). Of course, there is a reason for this. The first three requirements are in the line of obvious, if not of self-

[1] 2 Tim. 2 : 19.   [2] John 4 : 24.

evident, truths; the requirement of one day in seven for rest and worship is not, however, of obvious importance. Hence this requirement is specifically affirmed as an article of the covenant, while the others guard against departures from primal principles of vital moment.

The "Sabbath" was a recognized institution long before the days of Moses. Traces of its strict and sacred observance in the ancestral home of Abraham are disclosed in the Assyrian records unearthed in these later days. And now that the Lord, at Sinai, is drawing away his covenant people from the sins and errors of their fathers and neighbors, he reminds them that there is good in some of the observances of the past, which they are not to forsake or forget. "Remember," therefore he says, "the sabbath day to keep it holy"—as your fathers in all their polytheism had a care to observe it of old. Bear *that* institution in mind, as worth your remembering.

And here again there is affirmed a principle which is for all time and for all people. Although the reason for setting apart one day above another for rest and worship is not on the surface of things, the experiences of mankind, as well as the teachings of God's Word, go to show that there is such a reason below the surface. In the long run, man can do more work, and do it better, in six days of a week, than he can in seven; and unless a man worships God at stated times, he is not likely to worship him at all. So it is that God makes it a part of his loving covenant between himself and his people, that ever and always they shall worship him statedly, as well as worship him sincerely, spiritually, and solely; because without this stated recognition of the covenant, the covenant itself would be forgotten.

And now we come to the fifth of the ten covenant requirements: "Honor thy father and thy mother." This also is in the affirmative form, and for a very good reason. God is here declaring, as it were, that those who are in legitimate authority are so far his representatives. He wants it understood that while no other gods are in existence, even in a subordinate place in the universe, he has his representatives in various spheres of human government and rule, and they are to be honored accordingly by his covenant people.

We are accustomed to speak of the division of the Ten Commandments into two tables, the first comprising four requirements, and the second six; but it will be seen that this fifth requirement belongs with the preceding four in the group of those which look God-ward. It is as though the one table pointed upward from ourselves, while the other pointed outward. We are to honor those who are over us in the Lord, not as our fellows, but as our superiors; not because of what they are as men, but because they are, within the scope of their rule, the representatives of our God.

By Oriental custom the terms "father" and "mother" are by no means limited to one's natural parents, but are applicable to superiors in years, or in wisdom, or in civil or religious station. This truth was impressed on my mind by an incident in my journey across the desert of Sinai. My companions in travel were two young men, neither of them a relative of mine,—as my dragoman very well knew. When, however, in mid-desert, we met an old Arab shaykh, through whose territory we were to pass, my dragoman introduced me as the father of these young men. "No, they are not my *sons*," I said to the dragoman; but his answer was: "That's all right. Somebody must be father here." And when I found that, according to the Arab idea, every party of travelers must have a leader, and that the leader of a party was called its "father," I saw that it would look better for me to be called the father of the young men, than for one of them to be called my father.

Traces of this idea are found in the Bible use of the term "father." In Genesis, Jabal is said to be " the father of such as dwell in tents, and have cattle;"[1] the man who started the long line of nomad shepherds. Jubal is called "the father of all such as handle the harp and pipe;"[2] the pioneer instrumental musician of our race. Joseph in Egypt speaks of himself as "a father to Pharaoh,"[3] in view of the confidence reposed in him by the ruler of the empire. "Be unto me a father and a priest,"[4] says Micah to the young Levite, in the days of the Judges; because a religious guide is, in the East, counted as in a peculiar sense a representative of God.

It is not merely that the terms "father" and "mother" *may* include others besides human parents, but it is that no Oriental would think of limiting those terms to that relationship. Hence this fifth requirement of the covenant of God's people with their God, just as it stands, is in substance: Honor those who are over you in the Lord, as the representatives of the Lord; for the powers that be are ordained of God,[5] and he who fails to honor them lacks in due honor to him who has deputed them to speak and to act for himself. And herein is affirmed a principle which is as important to us to-day as it was to the Israelites in the days of Moses. Indeed, it may be

[1] Gen. 4 : 20.   [2] Gen. 4 : 21.   [3] Gen. 45 : 8.   [4] Judg. 17 : 10.
[5] Rom. 13 : 1.

questioned whether any precept of the ten covenant requirements has a more specific bearing on the peculiar needs of the American people, than this injunction to reverence those who are in authority because they are God's representatives in their sphere. Anarchy can have no tolerance in the mind of a child of God; but reverence for rightful authority has its home there.

Turning from the first table of the covenant with its upward look, to the second table with its outward look, we find that each new requirement in its order stands for a great principle which is applicable alike to all peoples and to all times, and which has its basis in man's loving union with God. The first of this series, the sixth of the ten requirements, is: "Thou shalt not kill;" or, "Thou shalt do no murder." Here is a great deal more than an ordinance forbidding the striking down to death of a fellow-man. Here is a call of God to guard sacredly the life of every child of God, as that which is dear to God. In the Oriental world, as in the primitive world generally, blood stands for life, and life is supposed to proceed from God and to return to God. When, therefore, an Oriental is told that he must not take it upon himself to shed another's blood, he realizes that that prohibition is equivalent to saying that it is not for him to decide when a life that God has given shall be recalled to God.

This idea it is that runs through the whole system of what is popularly known as "blood revenge" in the East. "Whoso sheddeth man's blood, by man shall his blood be shed: for in the image of God made he man,"[1] was the declaration of God as early as the days of Noah; and it is in the line of that declaration that any man in the East who sheds another's blood must surrender his own blood to the other's family, at the present day—as ever since the days of Noah. Not personal revenge, but divine equity, is the real basis of this system. Not because the life belongs to the man, but because it belongs to God, must it be guarded sacredly, and be accounted for—if taken away.

It is on this principle that the civil magistrate, as the messenger of God, takes the life of one who has taken another's life, in these days of the Christian dispensation. "He beareth not the sword in vain: for he is a minister of God, an avenger for wrath to him that doeth evil."[2] A child of God must count sacred every life which God has given; and except while acting as a specific messenger of God, he must never send back a human life to God.

[1] Gen. 9:6.   [2] Rom. 13:4.

The seventh covenanting requirement is a call to regard the family institution as an institution of God's appointing, and to refrain from aught that tends to its injury. "Thou shalt not commit adultery" means a great deal more than Refrain from unchastity because of its harm to yourself or to your neighbor. It means, Guard God's primal institution for man, as an institution which God holds dear. At the very beginning of the race, it was ordained of God that one man and one woman—the twain, not the three, or the four, but the twain—should be one flesh in loving union.[1] This institution of God's ordaining is dear to God, and it ought to be dear to every child of his; therefore God says to those who would be in loving compact with him, "Thou shalt not commit adultery." Because your and my interests are made one, you must not, you cannot, as my loving people, do aught that shall prove injurious to the family—to the institution which I have established, and which is dear to my heart.

This, again, is not an arbitrary commandment; nor is it one for a single period, or for a single people only. It is the enunciation of a principle which is vital to the well-being of all peoples at all times. It was so from the beginning, and it must be so unto the

[1] Gen. 2 : 24.

end. The family is the unit in the State and in the Church. It must not be ignored in the realm of society, of government, or of religion. He who would be true to God must be true to the institution of the family. And who shall say that we have no need of remembering this truth in our land and day?

The eighth requirement of the covenant guards the rights of property as within the plan and ordering of God. "Thou shalt not steal" is announced as an article of the loving compact of God's people with their God. Not merely because your fellow-man would object to your taking his property from him, but because the rights of property are of divine appointment, are you to refrain from claiming as your own that which now belongs to another.

This idea of regarding property rights as of God's appointment is peculiarly prevalent in the Oriental mind. The lines of tribal division in the desert are recognized as having divine sanction; and now, as in the days of old, it is hardly less than sacrilege to remove an ancient landmark in the East. Tribes which are at enmity will make raids across these border lines for purposes of plunder; but this is in the nature of what "civilized" nations call a "military necessity." Again, a stranger who enters a tribal domain without obtaining consent is treated as a smuggler, and all his property is confiscated accordingly. This, however, merely shows the primitive origin of the "high tariff" principle. Orientals who plunder from their enemies, or who collect impost duties from immigrants, do so in the belief that God sanctions these habits of the ages.

When one of the Arabs of our party, in crossing the desert of Sinai, found he had dropped a bag of meal, he went back to look for it, in perfect confidence that it would be left untouched by others. On my asking him if he had no fear that another Arab had carried it off, he replied that no Arab would steal from an Arab. Dr. Edward Robinson [1] saw a black tent hanging on a tree, where, as he was told, it had remained a full year awaiting its owner's return; and he says that if a loaded camel dies on the desert its owner draws a circle in the sand about it, and leaves it without any fear that it will be disturbed in his absence. Burckhardt [2] illustrates the estimate put by the Arabs on stealing, by the story of an Arab father who bound his own son hand and foot, and cast him headlong to death from a precipice, because the son had stolen from one of his tribal fellows. Life can only be taken at the call of God; but, according to this

---

[1] *Biblical Researches*, 11th ed., I., 142.
[2] *Travels in Syria and the Holy Land*, p. 475 f.

Oriental view, he who violates the property rights of one of God's children forfeits his very life to God.

The principle underlying this estimate of the sacredness of property rights, like every other principle enunciated in the Decalogue, is not an outgrowth of an arbitrary commandment, but it inheres in the very nature of God's dealings with the sons of men. What hast thou that thou didst not receive by God's consent?[1] What has thy fellow that he did not receive by the same permission? It is God who gives. It is for God to take away.[2] No loving child of God will refuse to heed the limits which his Father has assigned in the distribution of his possessions among the children of his love. That was the way in which the Orientals were taught to look at it. That is the way in which we ought to view it. Anti-property communism is rebellion against God.

Ninth in the list of the covenant requirements comes the summons to hold in sacred regard the personal reputation, or good name, of every child of God. "Thou shalt not bear false witness against thy neighbor" is a prohibition of slander, or of careless speech affecting the good name of one's fellow-man. This is not, as many have supposed, a mere injunction to truthful speech on all occasions. Lying needs no

[1] 1 Cor. 4 : 7.   [2] Job 1 : 21.

specific prohibition in a loving compact between God and his people; although the duty of truthfulness is inseparable from the thought of any compact with God—who could not be God if he were to approve untruthfulness.[1] But a disregard by man of the reputation of his fellow-man does need to be guarded against in such a compact; therefore its mention has a place here. A child's good name is always dear to his father. He who loves and honors the father will not be heedless of the reputation of the child. God is the Father of all. The good name of every one of his children is dear to him. He who loves and honors God will not be careless of the reputation of any one of God's dear children. Therefore it is that, in the loving covenant of God with his people, it is declared that love for God includes a truthful fidelity to the good name of every child of God.

How the application of this principle comes home to us in our social life as God's children! We are jealous of the good name of the members of our own families. We are tender of the reputation of those whom we know to be very dear to our dearest friends. But how careless we are of the good name of those in whom we feel no special concern, or of the reputation of those who happen to be personally disagreeable to

[1] Num. 23 : 19.

us! We hear and repeat the words spoken to their discredit without knowing whether or not those words are true. By our unguarded speech or looks we help, perhaps, to give a false impression to others concerning them. And all the while they are God's dear children, and every spiteful or thoughtless blow at them is a stroke at him. Is this consistent with our claim of loving union with their God and ours?

It was in the line of this principle that our Lord Jesus gave emphasis to his one new commandment, that those who loved him should love one another, as being dear to him;[1] and, again, that he declared that whoever ministered tenderly to one of his disciples should be reckoned as ministering to himself.[2] God links himself in loving sympathy with all his children, and he wants their welfare to be held dear by all who hold him dear.

And now we come to the tenth and last of the requirements of this covenant. Here we find an injunction that goes deeper than those which precede it on the second tablet of the written compact. "Thou shalt not covet." Not only, Thou shalt not openly disregard human life, or the family institution, or the property or the reputation of any one of thy fellows; but, Thou shalt not want to do any of these things.

[1] John 13 : 34.   [2] Matt. 25 : 40.

Thou shalt recognize thine own lot, and thy possessions, and the lot and the possessions of others, as God's assignment to thee and to them ; and thou shalt be contented within the sphere which he has deemed best for thee.

This requirement in the second table of the compact corresponds with the third requirement in the first table. The one says that the child of God must be sincere and unfeigned in his loving devotedness to God as his Father ; the other says that the child of God must accept in all heartiness his Father's ordering concerning himself, in his relations to all his brothers and sisters in the great family of God.

Here it is that we find the more spiritual teachings of the Decalogue concerning man's obligations to his fellow-man in the loving service of God, as they are pointed out, and emphasized in the words of Jesus, in what we call the Sermon on the Mount.[1] Here it is that the lesson comes home to us that it is not enough for us to refrain from actual murder and adultery and theft and false witnessing ; but that it is inconsistent with our devotedness to God as our loving Father for us to have a hateful thought toward one of his dear children ; for us to look longingly in the direction of another family assignment than that which is ours in

[1] Matt. 5 : 3 to 7 : 27.

the way of God's appointment; for us to turn a wistful or an envious thought toward any possession of another which we have no right to seek after. And all this is not of God's arbitrary commanding, but is in the very essence of God's loving covenanting with his chosen people. Therefore it is that the Apostle urges Christians to keep themselves from "fornication, uncleanness, passion, evil desire, and covetousness, the which is *idolatry;*"[1] the indulging in which is being untrue to God as one's covenant God.

And now in the light of these disclosures of the nature and meaning of the successive clauses of this covenant of God with his Oriental people, let us look back upon it as a whole in its spirit and teachings, in order that we may see what is covered by it, and wherein its applications are for us as well as for God's people of old. God must be recognized as God alone. No heart can love God as God, unless that heart loves God wholly. God must be worshiped spiritually; for spiritual things are spiritually discerned, and only as a man is lifted above sight and sense can he be in communion with the spiritual and the infinite. Union with God must be sincere and unfeigned; for only by a complete and willing surrender of one's

[1] Col. 3 : 5.

self can one's self be merged into a holy and infinite Personality. The loving worship of God must have its stated times, and hence, of course, its stated places, in order to have its fitting hold on the worshiper; and the recognition of this truth in the covenant is the authorization of all legitimate seasons and methods of worship. God's representatives in the family, in the State, and in the Church, are to be honored as God's representatives; and herein is the authorization of all right forms of human rule. These are the teachings of the first table of the covenant; and those of the second table are like unto them.

He who loves God must love those who are God's. As the Apostle expresses it: "If a man say, I love God, and hateth his brother, he is a liar: for he that loveth not his brother whom he hath seen, cannot love God whom he hath not seen. And [therefore] this [second] commandment have we from him, that he who loveth God love his brother also."[1] Every child of man is a child of God. Wayward and prodigal son though he be, he still is one who was made in the image of God; and his Father's heart goes out toward him unfailingly in love. Hence he who loves the Father must guard with sacredness the life of every child of that Father. He must honor the insti-

[1] 1 John 4 : 20, 21.

tution of the family, which is the human hope of the children of that Father. He must hold dear the property possessions and the good name of each and every child of that Father. And in his heart there must be such love for that Father's children as the children of his Father, that he will have no wish to do aught that shall harm any one of them in any degree.

Thus it is that the spirit and substance of the entire covenant compact stand out in those words of our Lord which lose their meaning if we look at the Ten Commandments as ten arbitrary commandings of God. When a certain lawyer came to Jesus with the knotty question, "Master, which is the great commandment in the law?" Jesus said unto him: "Thou shalt love the Lord thy God with all thy heart, and with all thy soul, and with all thy mind. This is the great and first commandment. And a second like unto it is this, Thou shalt love thy neighbor as thyself. On these two commandments hangeth the whole law, and the prophets."[1] And thus it is that we are enabled to realize that "love . . . is the fulfilment of the law."[2]

The "Ten Commandments" are the law, the law of the covenant of love; but, be it remembered, they

[1] Matt. 22 : 36-40.   [2] Rom. 13 : 10.

are not the "Mosaic law." They were not originated by Moses ; nor were they done away with when the Mosaic law was fulfilled and abrogated in Christ. They are the law of the promptings of love; an orderly statement of the principles which rule in a heart which is devoted to God. Their origin is in the nature of God ; and their continuance must be co-existent with the needs of the children of God. With all our shortcomings in love, and with all our failures in fidelity to our covenant-union with God in Christ Jesus, just so far as we are in oneness with God by faith shall we be true to the principles of this covenant-compact of God with his people. "God is love ; and he that abideth in love abideth in God, and God abideth in him."[1] "And hereby know we that we know him, if we keep his commandments."[2]

[1] 1 John 4 : 16.   [2] 1 John 2 : 3.

INDEXES

OTHER BOOKS BY DR. TRUMBULL

War Memories of an Army Chaplain
With 14 full-page Illustrations
Crown 8vo. $2.00

"This is incomparably the best chaplain's story which the great war has produced."—*Boston Journal.*

"Mr. Trumbull gives us no story, merely single incidents, and in them we find the tenderness and reverence and bravery and indomitable spirit of the American soldier. His book is throughout a eulogy of the American private soldier; the man upon whose patience and fidelity, obedience to superiors, and heroism the success of our arms must eventually depend."—*New York Times.*

"Chaplain Trumbull has given us an interesting volume, which is well worth reading, for its impressions have the stamp of truth, and he tells his story well."—*Brooklyn Daily Eagle.*

"It is safe to say that no chaplain in the Civil War was more widely known or did more effective service than the Rev. H. Clay Trumbull. . . . Add to this qualification the fact that Mr. Trumbull is a man of hearty sympathy, wide knowledge of human nature, and genial humor, and it will be concluded that this volume, called 'War Memories of an Army Chaplain,' is well worth reading. Emphatically it is so, and particularly at this time, when the subject of soldier life and the treatment of soldiers is so near to us. The book abounds in significant and entertaining incidents, and is thoroughly enjoyable from cover to cover."—*The Outlook.*

"Mr. Trumbull has given us a book upon the Civil War which is in some respects unique. . . . Mr. Trumbull's chapters on Religious Services in the Field, on Chapels, on Sermons, on Pastoral Work, are full of interesting matter."—New York *Evening Post.*

"This is an interesting and valuable work, not primarily historical in aim, yet casting upon the history of the Civil War a good deal of important light. . . . This personal record is as entertaining as it can be; parts of it are thrilling."—*The Historical Review.*

"A volume packed full of interesting reminiscences, anecdotes, and relations that bring back to us the war period from a fresh standpoint. Perhaps nobody knows as much about real army life as the regimental chaplain."—*Review of Reviews.*

CHARLES SCRIBNER'S SONS, Publishers
153–157 FIFTH AVENUE, NEW YORK

Other Books by Dr. Henry Clay Trumbull

CHARLES SCRIBNER'S SONS, Publishers

❦ ❦ ❦

The Blood Covenant
A Primitive Rite and its Bearings on Scripture
8vo. $2.50

"The facts are indisputable, and they tell their own story. Nor can we refrain from commending the volume as a most striking and valuable contribution to the religious thought of the world. It is emphatically one of the few books that no religious thinker can afford to be without."—*President* W. R. HARPER, *in the Old Testament Student.*

"We thank the author for this fruit of vast labor and persevering research. It is worthy of the study of all students of religion."—*Rev.* CHARLES A. BRIGGS, D.D.

"It seems to us to throw a true and important light upon the sacrament of the Holy Communion, and to rescue it alike from Roman perversion and Zwinglian degradation. Throughout we have been impressed by its reserve of power, its care not to press unduly any analogy. It seems to us a model of what biblical study should be."—*The Churchman.*

❦ ❦ ❦

The Threshold Covenant
Or, The Beginning of Religious Rites
8vo. $2.50

"It is brimful of accurate knowledge and new points of view, and is written so charmingly that a child could understand and follow."—A. H. SAYCE, *Professor of Comparative Philology at Oxford.*

"Un livre où s'allient à une si admirable familiarité avec les civilisations de l'antiquité tant de sagacité exégétique et de puissance de synthèse et d'invention."—*Revue de l'Histoire des Religions, Paris.*

"I am delighted to have been able to make early acquaintance with a book so full of facts which really illuminate the dark places of primitive times. That the explanation of the Hebrew Scriptures profits much by it is clear."—*Professor Dr.* T. K. CHEYNE, *Oxford.*

TOPICAL INDEX

AARON, God's covenant with, 17.
Ababde women, reference to, 99.
"Abusers of the salt," 110.
Added traces of the rite, 123-130.
"Agreement" used interchangeably with "covenant," 5.
Alexis, Grand Duke, reference to, 125.
"Ali Baba and the Forty Thieves," reference to, 254.
Altar and table as synonymous, 85.
"Ancient Mariner," reference to, 135.
Animal food supplies lack of salt, 38.
Antony and Cleopatra, reference to, 55.
Arabia, Bed'ween of, reference to, 110.
"Arabian Nights," reference to, 64.
Arabs: regard for salt covenant among, 29; not accustomed to put salt on table, 29 f.; rite of bread and salt among, 31; John Macgregor taken prisoner by, 32 f.; swearing by salt of, 54; milk sometimes accepted as substitute for salt by, 62; honesty of, 111 f., 166.
Archeology: its value compared with philology, 4.
Ark of the covenant, reference to, 145.
Armenians, supply of salt cut off, 43.
"Arrangement," used interchangeably with "covenant," 5.
Arvieux: cited, 34.
Asiatic cholera promoted by lack of salt, 46.
Asiatic Quarterly Review, reference to, 46.
Assyrian roots, gain of looking among, 4.
Assyrian: word for "salt," 76; words translated "covenant," 6 f.
"Attic salt," synonym of life in conversation, 68.

BABE: anoint with blood, 59; more life to a, 59.
Bancroft, H. H.: cited, 57, 95.
Band, symbol and pledge of union, 7.
Barley-meal cakes employed in sacrifice, 94.
Bartholow, Dr.: cited, 41.
Battas, in Sumatra, form of oath of, 123.
Bed'ween, conventions for covenants of, 30 f.

Bey, Durzee, reference to, 24.
Bheels, in India, reference to, 60.
Bible: references to the rite in, 17; carried over threshold of new house, 76, 106; estimate of treachery in, 113.
Bingham's "Antiquities:" cited, 89.
Bird Bishop, Isabella: cited, 47, 100.
Birth of child, salt at, 61.
Blackwood's Magazine, reference to, 127.
"Blood Covenant": reference to, 6, 7, 8, 9, 41, 45, 48, 53, 54, 59, 60, 62, 67, 79, 85, 86, 117, 118, 119, 120, 147.
Blood: fresh, drunk by people of Masaï, 37; salt representing, 37-50; drained from animals slaughtered by Jews, 39; transfusion of, 41; use of, as food, 41; red corpuscles of, 42 f.; saline ingredients in, 42 f.; anointing a new-born babe with, 59; Kaffir new chief washed in, 60; represented by wine, 117; atoned for by blood, 137; sprinkled by Moses, 148; shedding man's, 162 f.
"Blood-licker" in Mecca, 48.
"Blood revenge" in the East, 163.
Blunt, on Book of Common Prayer: cited, 80.
Bock, Carl: cited, 61.
"Boiling water, ordeal of," 101.
Booddhists in China, customs among, 92.
Bracelet as symbol and pledge of union, 7.
Brâhmanas, reference to, 90 f.
Bread: salt as an accompaniment of, 14; and salt, 23-34; significance of, 79, 80; and flesh, 119.
Bridal couple, sprinkled with salt, 128 f.
Browning, Mrs., quotation from, 55.
Buchanan, Dr., reference to, 41.
Bunge, Professor: cited, 38, 39, 123.
Burckhardt: cited, 24, 99 f., 100, 166.
Burder: cited, 31, 110, 112.
Burning Lamps, Feast of, 92 f.
Burning of salt, 99 f.
Burton: cited, 24; quotation from, 26.
Bush's illustrations, reference to, 109.
Buxtorf: cited, 87 f.

177

TOPICAL INDEX

CADAMOSTO, Aloisio, reference to, 69.
Cannibals, bathing body of chief in salt after death, 61.
Catacazy, Madame de, reference to, 125.
Ceres, reference to, 23.
Cattle, salt as meaning, 91.
Characteristics of a covenant, 3-10.
Chemist's use of term "salt," 39.
China: blood substitute for salt in, 38; depriving a person of salt a mode of punishment in, 42; customs among Booddhists in, 92.
Church, salt in dedication of a, 90.
Cicero, reference to, 68.
Circumcision as token of a covenant, 8.
Clapperton: cited, 24.
"College salting," 128.
Collitz, Professor Hermann, reference to, 50, 74.
"Compact," used interchangeably with "covenant." 5.
"Conventions," Bed'ween, 30 f.
Corpse, salt on a, in Scotland, 103.
Cosmas, reference to, 69.
Covenant: meaning of the word, 3 f.; characteristics of a, 3-10; etymology of, 5; words used interchangeably with, 5; marriage a, 7; circumcision as token of, 8; various kind of, 9, 13; Bible references in, 17s.
Covenanting, exchange of tokens and symbols in, 8.
Cross, sign of the, reference to, 89.
Curative powers of salt, 43 f.
Customs preceding words, 9.

DACIER, reference to, 70, 88.
Daraon, burning of salt among people of, 99.
Darius, King, directing supply from royal treasury, 20.
David, God's covenant with, 17 f.
Da Vinci's painting, reference to, 113.
Dead body, salt on breast of, 104.
Dead Sea, reference to, 58, 134.
Death: from *salts-hunger*, 42; salt used at, 61; or life, 133-138.
Dedication of a church, 90.
Definition, not easily reached, 5.
Delitzsch, Friedrich: cited, 7.
Denham: cited, 24.
Dhar, used in treaty of peace, 123.
Diab, Joseph, reference to, 28.
Discovery of salt as article of diet, 41.
Disputes settled by salt and water, 124.
Divination, salt in, 99-106.
Division of Ten Commandments, 159 f.
Doolittle: cited, 100.
Doughty: cited, 24.
Du Tott, Baron, quotation from, 27, 28.
Dyer, Thistleton: quotation from, 104; cited, 113, 137, 138.

EASSIE, W.: cited, 62.
Ebionites, salt and bread employed by, 50.
Edwards's "History of West Indies," quotation from, 60.
Egypt: salt forbidden to priests in ancient, 55; Feast of Burning Lamps in, 92 f.; burning salt in, 99; Muhammadan Arabs in, 100.
Egyptian: use of salt in sacrifice, 93; idea of wine and blood, 118; collection of taxes, 130.
Egyptians, table an altar among, 85.
El Hejaz, Bed'ween of, reference to, 110.
Elijah, reference to, 58.
Elisha, reference to, 57.
Elizabeth, Queen, reference to, 126.
Elkesaites, bread and salt employed by, 50.
Ellis's "History of Madagascar:" cited, 8.
England, burning salt in, 101.
Esquimaux, value of blood among, 39.
Etruscan: symbolism, 93; customs, salt in, 105.
Etymology of "covenant," 5.
Eucharist, salt in the, 89.
"Evil eye:" reference to, 100 f.; treatment received by James Napier for, 101 f.
Evil spirits, exorcising, 99.
Exactness of definition not to be reached, 5.
Exchange of tokens and symbols as a means of covenanting, 8.
Exorcism, salt in, 99-106.

FAITHLESSNESS to salt, 109-114.
"Father," Oriental meaning of, 160.
Feast of Burning Lamps, 92 f.
Fidelity to salt, 130.
Finn, Mrs., quotation from, 32.
"Fire: salted with," 65; salt leaping up in, 95; salt thrown into, 100.
Fish, salt in Dead Sea in lieu of, 58.
Flesh and bread, 119.
Flies, dead, life brought to, by salt, 63.
Flood, use of blood as food forbidden after the, 41.
Floor, salt sprinkled upon, 100.
Florus, reference to, 55.
Food: salt indispensable in, 14; use of blood as, 41.
Ford, George A.: cited, 101.
Founder of Saffaride dynasty, 27.
Fourmeaux, L.: cited, 40.
Frazer: quotation from, 110; cited, 118 f.
"Freshman, salting a," 128.
"Friendship the Master-Passion," reference to, 9.
Funeral, salt scattered at threshold after, 100.
Furness, W. H., 3d, reference to, 124.

TOPICAL INDEX 179

GERMANS, waging war for saline streams, 59.
German Jews, customs among, 86.
Gesenius: cited, 7, 109.
Ghoorka salt, eating, 110.
Ginger root, salt and, given as wedding-cake, 124.
God's covenant with his people, 150 f.
Gold, salt in exchange for, 69.
Greek Church, salt deemed essential in Eucharist by, 89.
Greek words translated "covenant," 7.
Griffis, William Elliot: cited, 47, 100.
Grimm, reference to, 74.
Gumpel, C. Godfrey: cited, 45.
Gypsies, Hungarian customs among, 129.

HALL, Bishop, reference to, 127.
Hamelin, M.: cited, 34.
Hamlin; Dr.: cited, 24.
Harmer: cited, 24.
Harper's Latin Dictionary, reference to, 94, 96.
Hospitality, salt symbol of, 126.
Hebrew roots, gain of looking among, 4.
Hebrew words translated "covenant," 6 f.
Hebrews, forbidden to eat "with the blood," 62.
Hehn, Victor; reference to, 69; quotation from, 70.
Hemorrhage, salt administered in, 40.
Henderson: cited, 103, 104, 137, 138.
Henniker, Sir Frederick, reference to, 49.
Herodotus: reference to, 92; cited, 119.
Hilprecht, Dr. Herman V.: cited, 76.
"Holy water:" salt essential element of, 90; and salt mingled in food and drink, 101.
Homer: cited, 53, 94.
"Honey, milk and," symbol of blood and flesh, 80.
Howell, W. H.: cited, 41, 42.
Hungarian gypsies, customs among, 129.
Hungary, wedding customs in, 128.

IAGO, reference to, 55.
Ideas precede words, 3.
Importance of salt in covenant, 32.
Infant, salt put into mouth of, 90.
Inspiration by wine, 118.
Intoxication by wine, 118.

JABAL, reference to, 160.
Japheth, reference to, 41.
Jastrow, Rev. Dr. Marcus: cited, 57, 86, 112, 137.
Jesus: references of, to salt, 64 f.; new commandment of, 169.
Jews: careful to drain blood from slaughtered animals, 39; observing covenant of salt at table, 84; table customs among, 87.

Josephus: cited, 83.
Jubal, reference to, 161.
Judas Iscariot, reference to, 113.

"KADESH-BARNEA," reference to, 58.
Kaffir chief, washed in blood upon assuming authority, 60.
Karna, reference to, 34.
Kauravas, reference to, 34.
Kluge: cited, 74.
Kohler, Dr. K.: cited, 88.
Kookies of India, treaty of peace among, 123.
Koordistan, salt lake in region of, 59.
Krishna, reference to, 34.
Kuhn: cited, 74.

LAISS-SAFAR, worker in brass and copper, 26.
Lane: cited, 24, 64, 100.
Lange, reference to, 65.
Layard: cited, 26.
Lea, Henry C.: cited, 101, 124.
"League," used interchangeably with "covenant," 5.
Lebanon region, blood covenant in, 48.
Leland, quotation from, 93.
Leprosy, prominence of salt as cure for, 45.
Life: dependent on salt, 42; salt representing, 53-70; seasoned with, 67; and light, 73-76; savor of, 133-138.
Light, life and, 73-76.
Livingstone, Dr. David: cited, 37 f., 38.
London Court Journal, reference to, 125.
London Quarterly Review, reference to, 43.
Lot's wife turned to pillar of salt,
Lying, reference to, 167 f.

MACGREGOR, John, experiences with Arabs, 32 f., 33.
Macrae, quotation from, 126.
Macrobius: cited, 49.
Madagascar, covenant of salt in, 34.
Mahabharata, quoted and cited, 33 f.
Man offered in sacrifice, 91.
Marie, Princess, reference to, 125.
Marriage: a covenant, 7; salt and bread placed under threshold at, 106.
Martène: cited, 101.
"Martyrdom of an Empress," 129.
Masai people, reference to, 37.
Meal, salt of the covenant not to be lacking from the, 18.
Meaning of the word "covenant," 3 f.
Means of a merged life, 141, 142.
Meat, eating of, as a pledge, 24.
Mecca, "blood-lickers" in, reference to, 48.
Mediterranean Sea, water not to be taken from, 70.
Merged life, means of, 141, 142.

Merrill, Selah: cited, 24.
"Merry Wives of Windsor," reference to, 55.
Message-bearer, salt in hand of, 126.
Meyer's commentary, reference to, 65.
Milk: substitute for salt, 62; used instead of blood, 62.
"Milk and honey" standing for blood and flesh, 80.
"Milk brothers," reference to, 62.
Money, salt as, 69.
Morier, James, reference to, 54.
Morris's "China:" cited, 92.
Morton, Dr. Thomas G.: cited, 41.
Mountains of salt, 70.
Müller, F. Max, reference to, 91 f.
Moody, D. L., reference to, 156.
Moses, reference to, 148, 158.
"Mother," Oriental meaning of term, 160.
Mount Sinai, Moses at, 148.

NAME signifying personality, 155 f.
Naming child, ceremony of, 124.
Napier, James: cited, 101 f., 104, 138.
Neptune, reference to, 23.
Nicoll, reference to, 65.
Niebuhr: cited, 24.
Noah: use of blood as food forbidden to, 41; reference to, 163.
Norwach: cited, 7, 14, 137.

OATH: Oriental form of, 54; different forms of, 123.
"Obligation," used interchangeably with "covenant," 5.
Old Testament, word "covenant" in, 18.
Oriental: form of oath, 54; meaning of terms "father" and "mother," 160; summit of treachery, 111.
Orientals, Bible written by, 146.
Othello, reference to, 55.
Oxford University, giving salt to students in, 127.

PAGE, Master, reference to, 54.
Pasha, Arabi, reference to, 130.
Pasha, Moldovanji, reference to, 28.
Paul, reference to, 67.
Perley, quotation from, 125.
Perpetuity, salt as symbol of, 84.
Perspiration, salt shown in, 40.
Philinus, reference to, 56.
Philology, archeology sometimes more valuable than, 4.
Pierrotti: cited, 24.
Plato, reference to, 53.
Pledge, eating meat as a, 24.
Pliny: cited, 45, 68, 70, 73, 94, 119.
Plutarch: cited, 23, 53, 54, 55, 56, 57, 119.
Poison of rattlesnake, 43.
Polo, Marco: cited, 69.

Preface to Ten Commandments, 150.
Price's "Mohammedan History:" cited, 27, 42.
Priests, salt forbidden to, 55.
Primitive covenanting, 6.
"Promise," used interchangeably with "covenant," 5.
Pythagoras: reference to, 70; quotation from, 88.

QUAIN'S "Dictionary of Medicine:" cited, 40, 62.

RALSTON'S "Songs of Russian People:" cited, 106.
Raphel, Don: reference to, 30; quotation from, 31; cited, 111 f.
Rattlesnake, poison of, 43.
Rawlinson's "Ancient Egypt," quotation from, 93.
Resuscitating drowned persons by salt, 63.
Richardson's English Dictionary, reference to, 96.
Ring as symbol and pledge of union, 7.
Robbery attempted by Yakoob, 26 f.
Robinson, Dr. Edward: cited, 166.
Rodd's "Customs:" cited, 101.
Rosenmuller: cited, 30; reference to, 54.
Russell's "Natural History of Aleppo," quotation from, 24.

"SABBATH," a recognized institution before Moses, 158.
Sacrifice on threshold, 47.
Sacrifices, salt in, 83-96.
"Sacrificial essence, the," 91.
Saffaride dynasty, founder of, 27.
Saffaride Kaleefs, story of the origin of the dynasty of, 26.
St. Augustine: cited, 89.
St. Peter, fresh water changed to salt by, 59.
Saïs, annual festival at, 92.
Salary, derivation of word, 68.
Saline injections, 40.
Salt: as preservative, 14; indispensable in food, 14; spoken of as an accompaniment of bread, 14; a vital element,-18; covenant of, perpetual and unalterable, 18; of the covenant not to be lacking, 18; in many lands the possession of government, 19; bread and, 23-34; nothing eatable without, 23; on a common table, 29 f.; importance of, to a covenant, 32; representing blood, 37-50; and salts, 39; discovery of as article of diet, 41; as antidote for snake-bite, 43; as saline ingredient of blood, 43; curative powers of, 43 f.; supply of, cut off from Armenians, 43; strewn on

TOPICAL INDEX

threshold, 47; representing life, 53-70; and sun, 73-76; in sacrifices, 83-96; in the Eucharist, 89; as sacrificial essence, 91; leaping up in fire, 95; in divination, 99-106; in exorcism, 99-106; not to be carried out of house after dark, 101; on a corpse in Scotland, 103; carried across threshold upon entering new house, 106; faithlessness to, 109-114; and ginger root given as wedding-cake, 124; water mocking thirst, 135.
Salt-cellar as point of division on family table, 126.
Salt-making, ordinary process of, 75.
Salted cake, essential in sacrificial offering, 94.
Salted water, drinking of, as a covenant, 48.
"Salted with fire," 65.
"Salting a freshman," 128.
Salts, salt and, 39.
Salts-hunger, death from, 42.
Samaria, woman of, reference to, 157.
Samoyedes dipping flesh in blood before eating it, 38.
Sanskrit roots, gain of looking among, 4.
Savor of death, 133-138.
Savor of life, 133-138.
Sayce, Professor A. H., reference to, 74.
Schrader, O.: cited, 74.
Schultz, Stephen: cited, 28, 29 f., 30.
Scipio, reference to, 68.
Scotland, salt on a corpse in, 103.
Scott, Sir Walter, quotation from, 127.
Seal killing by Esquimaux, 39.
Seasoned: with life, 67; with salt, 67.
Second requirement of God's covenant, 153.
Sentiment valuable in research, 5.
Septuagint, The, reference to, 33, 84.
Settling dispute by salt and water, 124.
Shallow, Justice, reference to, 54.
Shewbread, salt on table of, 84.
Shooter's "Kafirs:" cited, 60.
Sign of the cross, reference to, 89.
Significance of bread, 79, 80.
"Sin-eaters," reference to, 105.
"Sitting below the salt," 126.
Sixth requirement of God's covenant, 162.
Skeat: cited, 74.
Smith, George Adam, quotation from, 134.
Smith, W. Robertson: cited, 14, 24, 48, 59, 62, 137.
Snake-bite, salt as antidote for, 43.
Sodom destroyed because of faithlessness to salt, 112.
"Son" and "sun" from same root, 73.
Spencer, Herbert: cited, 123, 126.
Spilling of salt, 138.
Stanley, Henry M., reference to, 46 f.

Stealing, Arab estimate of, 166.
Stevens, Dr. W.: cited, 43.
Stewart's "Manual of Physiology:" reference to, 42; quotation from, 123.
Strassburg University, reference to, 128.
Strickland, Agnes: cited, 126.
Student, in Journal of Asiatic Society, giving salt to, 127.
"Studies in Oriental Social Life," 14, 23, 24, 58.
Substitute together with reality, 117-120
Substituting salt for blood, 37.
Sun, salt and, 73-76.
Supply of salt cut off from Armenians, 43.
Survey of Western Palestine, reference to, 32.
Swearing by salt, 54.
Sword, salt on blade of, 49.
Syrophoenician woman, reference to, 88.

TABLE: of shewbread, salt on, 84; an altar, 85; customs among Jews, 87.
Tacitus: cited, 135.
Tamerlane, Mongol-Tartar chieftain reference to, 109.
Tatar tradition of salt, 41.
Taxation in Egypt, 130.
Tears, salt shown in, 40.
Ten Commandments, division of, 159 f.
Thirst, salt water mocking, 135.
Thomson, W. M.: cited, 24; quotation from, 37.
"Three," value as sacred number, 103.
Threshold: pouring blood on, 47; Bible carried across, in new house, 76; salt and candle carried across, 76; salt scattered at, 100; salt and Bible carried across, in new house, 106; salt and bread under, 106.
"Threshold Covenant," reference to, 6 47, 106, 117, 128, 170.
Torture: depriving of salt as a means of, 42; treachery, Oriental summit of, 111; Bible summit of, 113.
"Treaty," used interchangeably with "covenant," 5.
Truce between enemies, sharing water as, 23 f.
Twain made one, 7.

VAN LENNEP: cited, 61.
Various kinds of covenant, 9.
Vegetable: diet used by those who take salt, 38; life, salt destructive of, 133.
Virgil, reference to, 94.
Volney: cited, 31.

WARBURTON: cited, 24.
Water: sharing of, 23; fountain of, cured, 58; not to be dipped from Mediterranean Sea, 70.

Wellhausen: cited, 95.
Wetzstein: cited, 24.
Wheeler's "History of India:" cited, 34.
Wilkinson's "Ancient Egypt:" cited, 93.
Wine: representing blood, 117; and salt, 119.
Wit, salt equivalent of, 67.
Woman of Samaria, reference to, 157.

Words: ideas precede, 3; limitations and imperfectness of, 3; customs precede, 9.

YAKOOB, a robber chieftain, 26.
"Youth, salt of," 54.
Yudhishthira, reference to, 34.

ZERUBBABEL, rebuilding of the temple by, 19.

SCRIPTURAL INDEX

GENESIS.

TEXT	PAGE
2 : 24	164
4 : 20, 21	161
9 : 4	41
9 : 6	163
17 : 1-14	8
17 : 14	114
18 : 1-8	120
19 : 24, 25	66
24 : 12-14	24
31 : 54	120
45 : 8	161
49 : 11	117

EXODUS.

TEXT	PAGE
3 : 8, 17	80
9 : 23, 24	66
13 : 5	80
20 : 1-17	145
20 : 2	150, 151
23 : 19	88
23 : 19 ; 34 : 26	62
24 : 7, 8	148
25 : 22	145
26 : 33, 34	143
29 : 40	119
30 : 6, 26	145
30 : 34, 35	84
31 : 7	145
32 : 15	145
33 : 3	80
34 : 26	88
34 : 28	149
34 : 29	145
39 : 35	145
40 : 3, 5, 21	145
40 : 20	149

LEVITICUS.

TEXT	PAGE
2 : 13	18
2 : 13	83
7 : 11-14	120
10 : 2	66
13 : 52-57	66
17 : 11	54
19 : 9, 10	88
20 : 24	80
23 : 12, 13	119
23 : 15-20	120

NUMBERS.

TEXT	PAGE
4 : 5	145
7 : 89	145
13 : 27	80
14 : 8	80
14 : 44	145
15 : 5, 10	119
16 : 13, 14	80
18 : 19	17
21 : 2, 3	137
23 : 19	168
28 : 14	119

DEUTERONOMY.

TEXT	PAGE
5 : 1-22	145
6 : 3	80
9 : 15	145
10 : 8	145
11 : 9	80
12 : 23	54
14 : 21	62
14 : 21	88
17 : 2-7	114
23 : 3, 4	24
24 : 19-21	88
26 : 9, 15	80
27 : 3	80
29 : 23	133
31 : 9, 25, 26	145
31 : 20	80

JOSHUA.

TEXT	PAGE
3 : 3, 6, 8, 11, 14, 17	145
4 : 7, 9, 18	145
4 : 16	145
5 : 6	80
6 : 6, 8	145
7 : 11-15	114
8 : 33	145

JUDGES.

TEXT	PAGE
2 : 20-23	114
9 : 45	134
17 : 10	161
20 : 27	145

1 SAMUEL.

TEXT	PAGE
4 : 3-5	145
25 : 10, 11	24

2 SAMUEL.

TEXT	PAGE
15 : 24	145

1 KINGS.

TEXT	PAGE
3 : 15	145
6 : 19	145
8 : 1, 6	145
18 : 4	24

2 KINGS.

TEXT	PAGE
2 : 19-22	58
18 : 11, 12	114

1 CHRONICLES.

TEXT	PAGE
15 : 25, 26, 28, 29	145
16 : 6, 37	145
17 : 1	145
22 : 19	145
28 : 2, 18	145

2 CHRONICLES.

TEXT	PAGE
5 : 2, 7	145
13 : 5	

EZRA.

TEXT	PAGE
4 : 14	20
6 : 8-10	20
7 : 21, 22	83
7 : 22	20

JOB.

TEXT	PAGE
1 : 21	167
22 : 7	24

PSALMS.

TEXT	PAGE
41 : 9	111
50 : 5, 16	142
55 : 19-21	114
107 : 33, 34	134

ECCLESIASTES.

TEXT	PAGE
39 : 26	117
50 : 15	117

ISAIAH.

TEXT	PAGE
24 : 5, 6	114
34 : 4	136

TEXT	PAGE
51:6	136
51:16	136
65:11	85
65:17	136
66:22	136

JEREMIAH.

TEXT	PAGE
3:16	145
11:5	80
11:9-11	114
17:6	134
32:22	80
34:17-20	114

EZEKIEL.

TEXT	PAGE
16:4	61
20:6, 15	20
41:22	85
43:21-24	83
47:11	134

HOSEA.

TEXT	PAGE
1:10	142
6:4-7	114
8:1	114

ZEPHANIAH.

TEXT	PAGE
2:9	134

MALACHI.

TEXT	PAGE
1:6, 7	85
3:2, 3	

1 MACCABEES.

TEXT	PAGE
6:34	117

MATTHEW.

TEXT	PAGE
3:12	66
5:3 to 7:27	170
5:13	65
5:13, 14	75
7:19	66
10:8	75
10:42	24
15:27	88
22:36-40	173
25:40	169
26:26-28	119
28:19	156
28:20	151

MARK.

TEXT	PAGE
7:7-11	137
9:41	24
9:49	65, 83
9:50	65
14:22-24	119

LUKE.

TEXT	PAGE
3:17	66
14:34	65
22:19, 20	119

JOHN.

TEXT	PAGE
1:4	76
4:9	24
4:24	157
13:18	111
13:34	169
15:6	66

ROMANS.

TEXT	PAGE
1:31	114
9:26	142

TEXT	PAGE
12:1	67
13:1	161
13:4	163
13:10	173

1 CORINTHIANS.

TEXT	PAGE
3:13-15	66
4:7	167
11:23-25	119

2 CORINTHIANS.

TEXT	PAGE
2:16	133
12:14	67

COLOSSIANS.

TEXT	PAGE
3:5	171
4:6	67

2 TIMOTHY.

TEXT	PAGE
2:19	157

HEBREWS.

TEXT	PAGE
9:19	148

1 PETER.

TEXT	PAGE
1:7	66

2 PETER.

TEXT	PAGE
3:10-12	136
3:13	136

1 JOHN.

TEXT	PAGE
2:3	174
4:16	174
4:20, 21	172

www.ingramcontent.com/pod-product-compliance
Lightning Source LLC
Chambersburg PA
CBHW032134160426
43197CB00008B/645